THE ROAD TO LIBERTY

Bringing an End to the 16th and 17th Unprincipled Amendments

Federico Lines
States Rights Radio

Paperback ISBN: 979-8-89238-512-1

Printed in the United States of America

16 17 18 19 20 21 XXX 9 8 7 6 5 4 3 2 1

Contents

FOREWORD

This American republic was founded by sovereign, independent states. The thirteen states came together to create a free society with a weak centralized government under the Articles of Confederation. In a few short years, however, the Constitution replaced the Articles with a strong central government with individual liberty protections in the Bill of Rights. Why?

As economist and historian Thomas DiLorenzo, author of *Hamilton's Curse: How Jefferson's Archenemy Betrayed the American Revolution,* pointed out in a 2008 essay:

> Hamilton was the leading advocate of a constitutional convention to "amend" the nation's first constitution, the Articles of Confederation. He lobbied for seven years to have such a convention convened, constantly complaining to George Washington and anyone else who would listen that "we need a government of more energy." Patrick Henry opposed Hamilton by sagely pointing out that the Articles of Confederation had created a

government powerful enough to raise and equip an army that defeated the British empire, and that that seemed sufficient to him.

At the convention, which scrapped rather than amended the Articles of Confederation, as had been promised, Hamilton laid out his grand plan: A permanent president who would appoint the governors of each state, and who would, through his state-level puppets, have veto power over all state legislation. A national government with the president given essentially the powers of a king is what he advocated. It was all rejected, of course, when the convention spurned Hamilton's nationalism and adopted a federal system of government instead, with only a few powers delegated to the central government by the sovereign states, mostly for foreign affairs. Hamilton subsequently denounced the new constitution as "a frail and worthless fabric."

In short, the American Revolution was supposed to leave it to the people and the states to the difficult task of self-government. Instead, the new Constitution was a betrayal of the principles of decentralism and state sovereignty. According to DiLorenzo,

> Jefferson and most other founders viewed the Constitution as a set of constraints on the powers of

government. Hamilton thought of it in exactly the opposite way — as a grant of powers rather than as a set of limitations — a potential rubber stamp on anything and everything the federal government ever wanted to do. He and his fellow nationalists (the Federalists) set about to use the lawyerly manipulation of words to "amend" the Constitution without utilizing the formal amendment process. "Having failed to persuade his colleagues at Philadelphia of the beauties of a truly national plan of government," Rossiter (Cornell University historian) wrote, "and having thereafter recognized the futility of persuading the legislatures of three-fourths of the states to surrender even a jot of their privileges, he set out to remold the Constitution into an instrument of national supremacy."

The Hamiltonian and Jeffersonian visions of America were fought over such issues as the First and Second Banks of the United States, taxation, debt, internal improvements, tariffs, and other issues that eventually led to the War Between the States, misnamed the Civil War.

President Lincoln embraced the Hamiltonian vision of America and imposed an excise tax–an income tax–to fund the Northern war machine.

He also created "greenbacks," paper money printed with green ink, to make up for tax shortfalls. Thus, the Constitution, which was claimed by some of its defenders to put checks on the newly created central government, failed its most important test. Instead of allowing the sovereign states to secede peacefully, Lincoln saw the Southern states as "cash cows" for the federal government because the tariff was the primary revenue source, falling heavily on the Southern economy.

Despite Lincoln's income tax disguised as an excise tax, which did not continue after the "civil war," the next attempt to impose an income tax occurred three decades later with the passage of the Wilson-Gorman tariff bill. The bill contained a "direct" income tax in violation of the constitutional provision that no federal tax "shall be laid, unless in Proportion to the Census or Enumeration herein directed to be taken." The Supreme Court ruled the income tax provision of Wilson-Gorman unconstitutional.

The 1895 dissent of Associate Justice John Marshall Harlan paved the way for the American progressive movement to lay the groundwork for the passage of the Sixteenth Amendment in 1913. This amendment is nothing more than thievery disguised as populism brought about by the unsavory and corrupt Senate characters who were elected because of the Seventeenth Amendment, further neutering the power of the states to create "more democracy" with the election of senators by popular vote instead by state legislatures.

The Sixteenth Amendment allows for a legal form of robbery – from national infrastructure spending, pork-spending projects on education, the arts, foreign aid, and the "untouchable" programs—Social Security, Medicare, and Medicaid.

The income tax was "sold" to the American people as a "rich man's tax, because only 2 percent of the public had to pay the tax. Four decades after its passage Frank Chodorov, author of *The Income Tax: Root of All Evil*, asserts that the income tax is indeed "evil" because it conflicts with the Ten Commandments.

...the Judeo-Christian tradition holds that in the field of morals all that is "good" is set down in the Ten Commandments, and that practices running counter to these dicta are "evil." There have been civilizations in which such practices as adultery, thievery, and even murder were looked upon as in the regular order of things, neither reprehensible nor praiseworthy, and in these civilizations the Ten Commandments, if known, would carry no weight. We can argue that our moral code makes for better living and is therefore superior to whatever went for a moral code in these primitive civilizations. That may be so. The point is that the Ten Commandments, though written in Heaven, had to be understood and accepted on earth before we could measure "good" and "evil."

Thus, the income tax—and the Federal Reserve created at the end of 1913—has made the welfare-warfare state possible. In short, the "revolution of 1913" was the culmination of the Hamiltonian vision for America and has cemented big government from "sea to shining sea."

The author of this book mentions that acts of corruption became more rampant after 1913, when the state legislatures no longer elected senators to represent them in the Congress. During the years of indirect election of senators, if there were issues of corruption, it was the concern of the individual state and not the national government. The matters of internal politics of a sovereign state need to be raised in the halls of each state legislature and not in the halls of the Congress.

The author explains how the federal government meddled in primary elections and decided to take the power away from the states. He explains in detail the 1921 primary elections in Pennsylvania and how the national Senate disavowed the will of the state, respectively the people, and acted against their senatorial representative. The expulsion of Sen. William Vare was an unconstitutional act and an attack on the sovereignty of all states, including the affected one, Pennsylvania.

There were only ten reported corruption cases in the pre-1913 era. Ten cases that were only rumors of potential corruption against the incumbent. The last alleged corruption case was in 1899. William Clark of Montana had no clear evidence presented against him or the state legislature. The progressive movement began making uncomfortable noises in the media that forced him to resign his seat.

In reading the Seventeenth Amendment, the author finds a distinct flaw in the language of the Vacancy Clause of the amendment. This unprincipled amendment took away the basic sovereign rights from the state legislature, or did it?

"Provided, That the legislature of any State "**may**" empower the executive thereof to make temporary appointments until the people fill the vacancies by election as the legislature may direct."

The author makes a valid point. The amendment has given the power to the state legislature to "may" or "may not" empower the executive to make temporary appointments. Therefore, the state legislature can take this power back and see fit to appoint an individual to the vacant seat and may or may not call for an election. It is all in the language of how it is established within the amendment. If the sentence had contained the word of "must" empower...," then that is a different story. There is sufficient evidence in calling for a repeal of this amendment and returning this power to the sovereign states.

The writer of this book is quite correct in saying, "That the Constitution cannot predict crooks, but the Seventeenth Amendment has indeed introduced it to the Constitution." Can it be argued that the passage of the Seventeenth Amendment created ethically challenged if not outright criminal behavior by such notable senators as Lyndon B. Johnson of Texas; Dennis DeConcini, Arizona; Alan Cranston, California; John Glenn, Ohio; John McCain, Arizona; Don Riegle, Michigan; and Robert Menendez, New Jersey?

That is the main problem that author Federico Lines sees: the advocates of limited government must fight the big fight, but also fight the little fights. "We the People" must rise to the challenge within our sovereign states and call for the state legislatures to take back their sovereignty by repealing the Seventh

Amendment. This would be a great step forward in giving the states more control over the federal government. Would this reduce the power of the federal government? We will only know if the original intent of the Founders is restored.

It was not a long hard battle for the progressives to literally turn the Constitution on its head in 1913. They used deceit and lies to amend the Constitution. What the author is trying to achieve in the following pages is to open our eyes to the deceit of what the progressive instituted. Federico Lines has outlined the best course of action for our nation.

I encourage everybody to be alert about the new laws and regulations, and the continued expansion of the welfare-warfare. New taxes and more are spending are on the table because the "beast" in Washington, DC needs more money to feed it and keep the beneficiaries of the welfare-warfare state satisfied.

America is at the proverbial fork in the road. With the federal debt at thirty-three trillion dollars at this writing and trillion-dollar budget deficits as far as the eye can see, the federal government is as dysfunctional as any family that is in financial crisis. The answer to the federal government's unsustainable financial policies can be found in this book. I strongly encourage you to read it and see what this author has to say how the roots of the welfare-warfare state that can be traced to the Sixteenth and Seventeenth Amendments.

Murray Sabrin, PhD
Emeritus Professor of Finance
Ramapo College of New Jersey
October 2023

I.

"The Senate of the United States shall be composed of two Senators
from each State, chosen by the Legislature thereof."

Article 1., Section 3., Par. 1.

"The Times, Places and Manner of Holding Elections for Senators and Representatives, shall be prescribed in each State by the Legislature thereof; but the Congress may at any time by law make or alter such Regulations, except as to the Places of Chusing Senators."

Article 1, Section 4, Par. 1.

Who does the upper house of the United States Congress truly represent? Does the Senate represent the state or the people? This was a question the progressives who established the Seventeenth Amendment never sat down and thought it through. They just changed the principles of the American republic with a complete disregard for the Constitution of the United

States of America. The progressive movement has always tried to derail our principles and establish its own agenda that goes against our American republic.

When the Founding Fathers convened at the federal convention to build a new Republic, they were being very careful in how to handle the representation of the constituents and the newly made states. They wanted everybody to have a voice in the small, but central government. The convention wanted two forms of representation, one chamber, the lower house, to represent the people and elected by the people. The second chamber, the upper house, to represent the states. They then asked themselves how the upper chamber members would be chosen to serve.

In this chapter, I am going to dictate erroneous errors in having a national senatorial electoral standard, instead of individual standards.

The convention came up with four ideas about how these members were to be picked: (1) appointed by the executive, (2) election by the people, (3) election by the lower house of Congress, (4) election by the state legislatures. As we now see, our Founding Fathers brought the idea of having the upper house Senate members elected by the people, a predicament we have today. But that was defeated because many of them had strong opposition to direct popular election of senators. From Thomas Pinckney of South Carolina to Roger Sherman of Connecticut, many shared a large voice of opposition. There was a small minority of people who supported direct popular elections. But their voice of support gave no heavy weight of strong evidence to pass such a measure.

Sherman voiced his opposition by saying, "The people immediately should have as little to do as may be about government. They lack information and are constantly liable to be misled." (George Haynes, *The Election of Senators*, 6).

If people believe this quote is pompous, then they truly do not understand the rules of federalism.

By reading this quote, I see where the progressives may find it pompous and seemingly autocratic, but it was nothing of the kind. He was right and fair. He stated that the people should not be as heavily involved in government, it never stated, "never involved in government." Sherman and other constitutional framers wanted the people to have some part in government and that is why they established the US House of Representatives. That is the sole people's voice in the general government of the United States.

The people, whether they are educated or not, will be misled by a rising populist political candidate or issues arising in the national government brought upon by fear. That is the current problem of populist ideals brought upon the direct representation in one House chamber, now with two, it has been chaotic. Even before the enactment of the Seventeenth Amendment, you had national populist politicians, whether in the US House or as President, inflicting fear and mistrust upon its people. The 1816 Tariff Act is one example. But the biggest misleading liability towards its people was the Forced Bill of 1832. This bill increased the size of the federal government, the President's power through the military, commerce, and taxation.

The Forced Bill of 1832 was a bill that bestowed fear by the President and several members of the U.S. House of Representatives, but not members of the national Senate. At least one Senator spoke against it, from the sovereign state of South Carolina. In those days, the National Senate stood tall for federalism and against populism in the national arena of our Republic. Therefore, it is and was quite important that the national Congress maintained its separation of representative power, and independence from the other branches of the national government. And separated within the sovereign several States.

Elbridge Gerry of Massachusetts, a former vice president, stated something that you would find in James Madison's Federalist #63. "To draw both branches of the legislatures from the people would leave no security to the latter [the commercial] interest; the people being chiefly composed of the landed interest, and erroneously supposing that the other interests are averse to it." If you are familiar with Madison's Federalist #63, you would take note that he also takes under consideration that with too much representation to the people, their interests will become blinded by other interests set forth by their popular elected representatives and national senators. To share equal representative power, the divisions of a representative government must be accurately well developed, to maintain a stabilizing healthy republic. This is one of the primary reasons that the framers were so adamantly in support of a people's representation and a state's representation.

> The people can never willfully betray their own interests; but they may possibly be betrayed by the Representatives of the people; and the danger will be evidently greater where the whole legislative trust is lodged in the hands of one body of men

than where the concurrence of separate and dissimilar bodies is required in every public act.[1]

Pickney of South Carolina lent his great voice of opposition to this measure. It is a shame that in 1913, nobody used his writings to go against the measure, titled the Seventeenth Amendment. He asserted that an election of either branch to be elected by the people, scattered as they were in many states, particularly in South Carolina, was totally impracticable (Haynes, *The Election of Senators*, 5).

The Founding Fathers knew that this new nation will indeed grow, and these states did grow. They were already counting into the fact the population growth in each state. Back in those days, the states of New York and Pennsylvania were larger in population compared to states like South Carolina and Virginia. They were indeed thinking of correct proportioned representation for both chambers especially for the Senate. The upper house membership cannot be consisted

---

1 James Madison, —No. 63: The Senate Continued, in Clinton Rossiter, ed., The Federalist Papers (New York: Mentor, 1999), 380-88.

with members from one state with a population of over ten million citizens and the other state with a population with over ten thousand citizens and still with a two-member Senate delegation elected by the people. That was not the idea of this chamber to begin with. This chamber was to represent the needs and interests of the state's growth, not the population growth. The lower house was responsible for the needs and interests of the population growth.

And so, a consensus was reached at the federal convention through an agreement by a majority that the election of senators would be through their own state legislatures. R. D. Spraight of North Carolina was the first to propose such a motion.

Elbridge Gerry of Pennsylvania made another point about the direct popular elections of senators. He stated, "I would be more contended that the commercial and moneyed interests would be more secure in the hands of the state legislatures than of the people At Large" (Haynes, *The Election of Senators*, 9-10).

Gerry makes a valid and true point. After 1913, the popular election of senators has always been competing on the idea to "bring the money to the people." One case that I bring into mind, was the 2006 Montana senatorial election between Republican Senator Conrad Burns and Democrat challenger Jon Tester. Burns' main campaign slogan was "Delivering for Montana." Senatorial candidates from both political parties after 1913 have become people pleasers rather than "state pleasers" and that simply was a direct blow to the Founding Fathers' principle of the upper chamber's representation.

The vote finally came for a state legislature election of senators and only two states, Pennsylvania, and Virginia, voted against it. The other nine states voted in favor, and it passed. The beginning of the States' representation in the National Congress became a reality. While the people maintained their representation in the other House of the National Congress. The US Representatives has a constituency to represent them, and the national Senator has its state as its constituency.

From 1788 to 1861, the sovereign States obtained their independence and sovereignty from the national government. There were times indeed the general government of the United States, whether the executive, with the National Congress and the high court ruled in favor for centralized autocracy over State sovereignty.

The best examples that I can give you have been with the Tariff Act of 1816 and the Tariff Act of 1832, also known as the Forced Bill of 1832. With the tyrannical presidency of Andrew Jackson, the federal government saw an opening to expand their power through unconstitutional measures.

Even after, the presidency of Andrew Jackson ceased to exist after his two full terms, the stench of federalized autocracy continued to be more rampant than ever. Article V of the United States dictated that "No State shall be deprived of its equal senate representation without its consent." If there was more violations of Article V and the Tenth Amendment to our Constitution, then it was during the terms after Jackson but also mostly during his reign of terror. And most national Senators stood up not only against Tyrant Jackson but afterwards.

One was the favored son of South Carolina, Senator John C. Calhoun that fought against the tyrannical policies of Andrew Jackson and later in his years. He truly represented his state constituency against the federal government. He fought hard to fight against the federal direct taxation policies onto his state and its several other sister states.

"I go on the ground that this Constitution was made by the States; that it is a federal union of the States, in which the several States still retain their sovereignty." (John C. Calhoun)

As all sovereign states stand with their sovereignty, so goes their national representation in the national senate. And their representation must demonstrate strong with this sovereignty. It must repel any inclination of favoritism and privilege being instituted by the federal government. The representation in the Senate must resist all kinds of privilege from the federal government, but they also must resist all forms of agitation and force from the national government.

The American public saw an invasion of state sovereignty and agitation, but also giving privilege to other States. In 1850, the National Congress passed a despicable, unjust, and unconstitutional law onto the several States. They passed a law titled, the Fugitive Slave Act. This law was entitled to be an act of dangerous proportions towards the independent, sovereignty of the several states of our American republic. It was supposed to give privilege to the several states that had slavery policies in their laws and assistance from the federal government. Even in where other several states had anti-slavery laws, those pro-slavery several States had the authority to enter that state and recaptured

One who increases the size of the national government, increases his ego for personal and ambitions reasons and interests.

the slave that escaped from their home property. In some states, they denied being of assistance and cooperation with federal union officials, which is their sovereign independent right to achieve.

I am not a man to support the institution of slavery, or an advocate of violence to bring national attention against this issue. I am a proponent of the use of federalism to curtailed and destroy this institution from the sphere of thinking in America.

For the national government give a scent of privilege to the sovereign states, mostly in the South, and deny the rights of many northern states, is a strict violation of the Constitution and rules that bind this republic. We all must respect the sovereignty of all the several states.

The sponsor of the legislation was famous in its name but not famous in federalism integrity like his grandfather had. He was James M. Mason, grandson to a famous framer to our Constitution, George Mason. As a son of the great sovereign Commonwealth of

Virginia, which is gathered with other great sons of Virginia. He instituted policies of centralized autocracy; a faction heavily opposed by those sons of Virginia. In supporting a law like the Fugitive Slave Act, he further moved to increase the size of the federal government, rather than decreasing or maintaining it small. One who increases the size of the national government, increases his ego for personal and ambitions reasons and interests.

To further increase your personal interests while increasing the size of the central government will place you in a dark section of our American history. While serving in the national government, especially in this nation, we must all curtailed to respect our neighboring sovereign states in conducting business for the protection of our Constitution. And Senator James Mason regrettably did not curtail to that respect and instituted his own greedy agenda of Virginia and Virginia businesses onto the agenda of Wisconsin and other States.

To bring up the word of God and talks of protection of slavery by way of religion into the Halls of Congress is a violation to our Constitution. While preaching for the violent act that was slavery. Slavery was an immoral institution imposed by a dangerous condition of privilege granted by the federal government.

One thing, that I despise, my fellow readers is when a national politician invokes a popular or religious rhetoric to also move his personal agenda further. The national Senate is not a place for populist rhetoric. The national House of Representatives is the place for populist rhetoric because they are being elected by a populist constituency.

As I despised Andrew Jackson when he used populist rhetoric as he supported his tyrannical policies, I am keen to despise more national senators in using this tactic. Mason and fellow men in those days and currently, are using the protection of the federal government to protect their interests. Calhoun died before this law came into effect, but I strongly believe he would have opposed it. Calhoun was no man of hypocrisy and as he supported for all States to retain their sovereignty, then this law would be a violation of that sovereignty. Calhoun was Mason's mentor but sometimes the protégé obtains more radical ideas than the mentor. I believe that is what happened to James Mason.

If the high court would have granted the right to the sovereign State of Wisconsin, the right to grant freedom and citizenship to any resident residing in that State. I have confidence, the civil war of 1861 would not have come to existence or would not have become a bloody and lengthy conflict. If the national Congress did not respect the sovereignty of Wisconsin, then why would the high court have shown any difference. Especially when the Chief Justice of the high court at that time was a native of a slave-holding State and proponent of centralized autocracy.

Slavery would have ceased to exist if the national government did not meddle to protect it. And if senators from those slave-holding States would have respected the sanctity of humanity and the sovereign right of those non-slave holding States. Now, national Senator Charles Sumner of Massachusetts, and men like him, were not men of strong federalism values but at least they stood against the inhumane policy of slavery.

These are dangers of when national politicians in the Senate get too much of a populist ideology. They forget their true representation and seek more in the outer realms of their state's representation.

The Fugitive Slave Act was a real test upon the actions and inabilities of how a state must behave in this republic. If a state is reserved to respect the laws and rights of their own state, then it must be set to be reserved to respect the laws and rights of the other several states. That respect is granted by the state's representation in the national Senate. The actions of Representative Preston Brooks against Senator Charles Sumner were an unfortunate turn of events that further angered the sanctity of the

American republic. Preston Brooks, a member of the lower house of the national Congress attacked a fellow member of the upper house of the national Congress without provocation and insisted agitation, only because of difference of ideas and views. America is a nation that was supposed to have been a heavily influenced and evolved nation around the world. To show the world that we would not allow ourselves to be governed by a centralized autonomy or protective custody techniques and tactics. To see a fellow American beaten mercilessly another fellow American, shows lack for advancement to be a great nation among the rest.

Because of this unfortunate institution of its history, now we rely more into the grasps of the national government. And once the esteemed national upper house of the nation's Congress has reluctantly become a haven of centralized masses that paved the way of a now democratic unity of dependent states, rather than a representative unity of sovereign states.

The national Senate was the haven to protect the sanctity of our republic from furthering the advancement of a sole centralized government autonomy or cooperation with that autonomy for whatever issue derived. Slavery plagued this republic but with autocratic plagued minds, the issue grew stronger by invading the rights and sovereignty of the several states.

This act is what led to the armed conflict of our republic. For the national government to pursue that one sovereign state is above the law to others leads to control and loss of independence for all. Sadly, with the arrogance of members in the national senate, mostly in the southern sphere, proved nothing but ignorance, rogue, and arrogance. What lead after the bloody conflict in result of this federal law, was more interference from the federal government. Not only in the realm of civil rights, which became added amendments, but unconstitutional power granted in other areas by the national government to set themselves to control.

No sovereign state is above any other state. As they are all equal under the law, as it is defined in the Constitution. If only James Mason and others like him would have comprehended the rules of federalism and applied them, while rejecting the rules of vanity and arrogance. America could have succeeded to be a true representative republic. Even to this day, I will call on the national Senate delegations of each of the several states to stand by their own state and stop meddling in other state's affairs. And to stop using the national Senate as their own bully pulpit. The national Senator is there to further advocate for their state's rights and sovereignty but with accordance to the Constitution and the along the rights of humanity.

From 1789 up and until the disgraced moment in American history known as the Civil War and to 1913 the states had a representative chamber in the national government. The people had their representation as well. One Senator David B. Turpie of Indiana (1887-1899) pointed out the distinct and grandiose opinion of the national Senate:

> "The state legislatures during the War of Independence and for and for some time afterward were the favored and trusted depositories of a variety of delegated powers. It is not strange, therefore, that the part given them in the election of members of the senate should have attracted little notice, elicited no dissent." (Haynes, *The Election of Senators*, 18).

The delegated powers of the national Senate were indeed enumerated and not to be handled with abrupt decisions against the several States of our union. The only difference is when the national Senate began to have populist traits due to the direct election of this chamber, new unconstitutional powers came with this electoral appointment.

Senator Turpie did point out the dangers of what the national Senate was to become, and we are now suffering because of a sole amendment for centralized power.

Before we get into the disgraced ruin of the national Senate electoral decision game changer, let's look at how the federal government after the Civil War changed it for us by instituting new rules for a centralized autonomy. The States in rebellion were once again readmitted into the union of sovereign States. They reentered to a new era of this nation. A new era of a futuristic centralized autonomy. The northern states did not trust most of the southern states and therefore with a majority in the national Congress imposed new and unconstitutional rules.

There were several states that never had a full delegation in the national Senate due to their own state constitution and procedures. A couple of examples come to mind. The California state legislature sometimes found it difficult to elect Senators, notably in the elections of 1851, 1855, and 1856. The state of Indiana for a brief period only had one Senate delegation representing the Hoosier state. But this was meant to happen since this country was built on individual states with their own autonomy. If the state legislature did not get their act together in sending their full state delegation to the national Senate to conduct business on their state's behalf, then it would be the state's problem and the state legislature would face difficult reelection. But the other states that did follow the national Senate's session schedules should never have been punished just because of a few states' tardiness. And part of this issue, came a legislation that was "the beginning of the end to our American republic." An act was established to make rules for states to fully choose their Senate delegation in time before the national session of Congress.

The Act of 1866, an act to regulate the times and manner of holding election for Senators in Congress. The language of the choosing of national senators seemed a bit vague. Does the Congress have a right to regulate the times and places of how a senator is elected by the state? In my humble, honest constitutional scholar mind, they do not have that right or power. The Congress has the power to regulate the rules of the chamber's assembly. But as to how a sovereign state chooses their Senator, that power resides within each sovereign state legislature.

This act brought the end to our states' representation and self-governing sovereignty and autonomy. The beginning of central government intervention. Briefly what this act states are that no state legislature will be left behind in electing their full Senate delegation in time for the session in the national Senate. This legislation came just after the Civil War during the Reconstruction. The radical Republicans in power wanted to control the rebel states and their state legislatures in how to elect their Senate delegation. I guess these radical Republicans did not want any more secessionist (Democrat) senators. One region was ruined by the aftermath of war, but these legislators ruined an entire principle of the nation. Like I have stated before, if a state legislature misses the deadline to elect their Senate delegation in time to be represented in that year's national session, then it is too bad for that state. Those state legislators would have had to answer to their voters on their election days for missing these deadlines.

Since the Act of 1866 was passed, we have witnessed more chaos and disharmony brought upon the upper house of our nation's Congress and in our republic. Since the state legislatures were ordered by a central government legislative mandate to pick their Senate delegation before the national session, the breakout of deadlocks came into play. From 1867 to 1913, there were thirteen deadlocks in numerous state legislatures and almost twenty states affected (Haynes, *The Election of Senators*, 40).

Due to these deadlocks, the state legislatures were more focused in picking a senatorial delegation than taking up issues of their own state. I am going to cite two different state legislatures that had an issue of electoral deadlock battles.

In Tennessee, in 1898, the state legislature of the Volunteer state had begun the process and balloted eighty-six times for their senatorial candidate before the session would have begun. But it wasn't until the 145th ballot in the caucus that Mr. (Thomas) Turley was nominated; yet the official record of the assembly stated that he was elected on the seventh ballot and gave no indication of the bitter conflict which had made his triumph possible. In North Carolina, 1903, the senatorial election was affected upon a winner not until the sixty-first ballot and Lee Slater Overman won the nomination. This was the result of the 1866 Act. The legislators were forced to argue ballot after ballot even though by the third or fifth ballot, they would have picked a nominee (Haynes, *The Election of Senators*, 42-43).

There was only one scandal of bribery and corruption before the unconstitutional Act of 1866. It happened in 1857, in the state of Pennsylvania. The Pennsylvania state legislature chose Simon Cameron to be their senator but there were certain members that disapproved and presented a case of "by corrupt and unlawful means" of the Cameron pick. (Haynes, *The Election of Senators*, 53).

A Senate committee was called to investigate these charges. The Senate committee made their report known that the allegation was entirely too vague and indefinite to bring forth a criminal allegation against this case. The Senate committee also presented in their report that if a protest of this nature was backed up with a responsible source, the senate should investigate the charges and allow the protestors to submit the (valuable) evidence (Haynes, *The Election of Senators*, 54).

You are always going to find disgruntled people who are going to scream "wolf," and yet there is nothing there. When the radical progressive movement, regardless of political party wants radical change, they will always find a scapegoat of a person or issue, spin the issue to their own special interest and invoke unconstitutional change. This was one case, and yet after 1866, there were several cases brought upon the Senate on the issues of bribery and corruption.

From 1866 to 1899, there were rumblings, only rumblings, of acts of corruption among several state legislatures, but no one came forward and the Senate committee found no concrete proof of these actions up until 1899. The Montana state legislature appointed William A. Clark to be their senator in the national

Congress. Apparently, a Senate committee received reports that there were acts of bribery and corruption of state legislators involving Clark's appointment including the nominee himself. The Senate committee reported that eight votes were obtained through illegal bribery acts. This case was argued extensively in the Senate, and it was ended when Clark resigned from his seat after a lengthy speech to proclaim his defense that he made on the Senate floor (Haynes, *The Election of Senators*, 55-56).

After the scandal of 1899 broke the news, state legislators and national legislators got scared. They imagined that they too would suffer the wrath of bribery and corruption and they decided to alter the principles of this country to benefit themselves.

The 1899 incident brought down a single individual with corrupt tendencies. Whatever happened to the eight individuals and the rest of the Montana state legislature who were also reported to have had some sort of a bribery/corruption activities with the nominee Clark went dismissed and no action was taken. An entire nation suffered a wrath of unconstitutional proportions to a political gossip tale of filled legends of corruption, and yet, there was no credible evidence to that effect. These progressive legislators took the easy way out of cutting out the corruption of American politics. Instead of rooting out the corrupt individuals that let Clark into the Senate, they altered the Constitution to please their own personal indulgences.

Because of this sole reported case, the movement increased for the national senate to change from its own sovereign standard to a national senatorial electoral standard.

In the next chapter, I will show you the examples, more than just the 1899 incident, of the product of this unprincipled amendment that led to more corruption and disgrace to our national legislative institution.

"The present scheme of congressional representation was widely planned. Nothing more plainly marks the tyro in politics than his eagerness to secure radical changes in existing institutions without first whether the alleged abuses find their real source in the institution which he assails; whether the remedy he proposes is appropriate or adequate, or whether its application will produce disorganization and other evils worse than those which it aims to remove. To prove that the Constitution of the United States should be so amended as to provide for the election of senators by popular vote, it is not enough to point out deplorable defects in the Senate: it must further be proved that these defects are due to the present method of election, that popular elections are calculated to remedy the evils and to do so without causing disproportionate injury to the structure and working of American government" (Haynes, *The Election of Senators*, 211).

"The scheme of representation in Congress is no hazard affair which slipped into the Constitution by accident. It was the subject of long and anxious debate on the part of the members of the Federal Convention, who insisted that ever essential interest should be given adequate consideration. They therefore adopted the plan of a bicameral legislature, with the two houses chosen upon different bases, the House standing for population, while the Senate represented States as such. This bicameral system, together with the long term and gradual renewal of the Senate, secures a representation of both the radical and the conservative tendencies such as is essential to the progress of every great democratic state. Moreover, there comes to the Senate a degree of independence from the very fact of its election from a source other than that of the representatives, which is highly essential to its exercise of a salutary check upon the House (Haynes, *The Election of Senators*, 211-212).

The framers of the Constitution did not plan this overnight without truly thinking in how to establish these two different of representative chambers for the national Congress. In theory and in practice, the idea of this bicameral system works best in a republic that is true in trying to seek a federalism style of government. The national Senate does indeed give a clear representation of both type of tendencies of ideas from radical to conservative. Its main purpose of this balance is of course a clear representative form of governance by each of the chambers.

"It is often implied that the election of Senators was put in the hands of the state legislatures merely because with the then crude means of communication, popular elections were impracticable" (Haynes, *The Election of Senators*, 212).

Popular elections are only impracticable if it was never set up to be decided by the masses. There was a reason that the national Senate was made clear that the deciding factor was the state legislatures. But to perfectly frank, popular elections are not impracticable, they are unpredictable and unstable.

Therefore, the presidential elections are not decided by a popular election. They are decided by the American electoral college and the procedures and standards are set up by the several states in accordance to Article II, Section I, Clause II. Imagine if those elections would be decided by the popular masses, we will never hear the end of it with runoffs after runoffs. So, to put it an end of discussion for the Trumper movement of 2020, it is the electoral college who decides the President, not the popular vote.

"But the legislature is thoroughly representative of the State" (Haynes, *The Election of Senators*, 214).

They are the state representatives of each voter and therefore elected by each voter. Then appointing a national Senator is just like voting for a legislation.

Legislative election was adopted because, under the conditions then prevailing, it had proved itself a serviceable method in many and varied applications; and not one word in the Convention's debates implied that the legislatures had abused this power. In fact, members of the Convention showed not so much a contemptuous distrust of the people, as a little wholesome knowledge of themselves, and of men whom they represented. They knew, as Senator (George Frisbie) Hoar (of Massachusetts) has said, that "although every Athenian citizen might be Socrates, every Athenian assembly would still be a mob." The Constitution, therefore, deprecated the immediate action of the people, in order that they might not "wed Raw Haste, half-sister to Delay." The framers of that instrument of government had more courage than many of their modern critics, for they had enough faith in the people to dare to appeal to their self-control. "They trusted the people with a profound and implicit trust when they submitted to them constitutions, both state and national, filled with restraints which alike secure minorities against majorities, and secure the whole people against their own hasty and inconsiderate action" (Haynes, *The Election of Senators*, 214-15).

The whole illusion to create that legislative senatorial appointments are a distrust of the people is nonsense to the extreme lying of the then-progressive leaders. The national senate chamber was never intended to be filled in by influence of the plebs. "Although every Roman citizen might be a Cato, every Roman assembly would still be a proper gathering." This is the motto that this republic aspires to be in the colonial era to the modern twentieth century era.

When you impose "trust" onto the people for making these difficult decisions and expect to obtain good actions after the fact. Direct popular elections in the national Senate will and has created differences between the majorities and minorities of groups and influences. That alone has suffered the wrath of whoever holds the majority while putting down the minority. Even though the majority party in 1850 was the Democratic Party, and they were able to achieve to pass the unconstitutional Fugitive Slave Act. The minority party across the national Senate and in the several states were able to refuse to cooperate and resist the evils of a federal act of the national Congress.

I am not including the popularly elected national House of Representatives because even though the minority of that chamber would also stand against this act of Congress and other acts that were deemed not holding with the Constitution. But the national Senate is the key in maintaining an indirect pipeline and clear communicate with the several states because the responsibility lies with the state legislature to achieve to protect the sanctity of their state. Nowadays, the majority holds the power, and the minority is useless because of the direct populist idea that whenever the majority obtains control, they will install fear and the thought of a national protective custody police authority. Then the minority in the national Congress cannot even organize in their own several sovereign state the need of refusal legislation for the very thought that they will be reprimanded. After the Fugitive Slave Act, a citizen, a legislator still felt that could be deprived of their private life and possessions. But the fight was still there to obtain victory against the majority oppressor and the very idea of instituting nullification legislation.

The very thought of nullification legislation in today's American political world has become non-existent. The tool to fight to preserve to maintain and protect our federalism republic has been violently opposed by the federal government and now we are beholden to support whatever federal legislation comes to mind with no sense of constitutional regard.

Nullification was a tool used by the national Senate, prior of the unprincipled idea of direct election of senators. It was a tool for the states to retain their sovereignty in the national government. People must remember that a national senator has an ambassador status, representing their state. This was not your typical definition of an ambassador. It was not to be a position of diplomacy but a position of respect to be respected by the national government and among their national senate colleagues. If disagreement occurred in the national Senate, proper distinguished decorum was always the proper attitude in that chamber. The strategy of nullification was popularly accepted by the residents of the states:

> The people of Carolina believe that the Union is a union of States, and not of individuals; that it was formed by the States, and that the citizens of the several States were bound to it through the acts of their several States; that each State ratified the Constitution for itself, and that it was only by such

> ratification of a State that any obligation was im-
> posed upon its citizens. (John C. Calhoun, *Against
> the Force Bill*, 1833).

I can only speak from my research on one Senator that he spoke for his sovereign State and against the unconstitutional grabs of the federal government. I strongly believe that all citizens of all the several States entrust that this republic was a union of States and not of individuals. And it is not a union of centralized governance.

And since it is a union of the several States, then the representative body of the national senate must be represented by the senators, electorally appointed by their state legislature.

When will the residents of each sovereign State finally comprehend that the national senate is the legislative tool for the states' business while the national House of Representatives is the people's business? Giving too much attention via-a bicameral system of government to the people will lead to a narcissistic-personality complex of citizens. The requirement of attention will increase, and the amount of special interest favors will be astronomical, also the amount of disappointment will be astronomical. I find that the state legislators and national senators of the past were not as disappointing as the ones today. They never curried for any special interest favors for the residents, only the interests of the State.

This is one lie that the progressive will gladly tell the nation that it is the opposite. But nothing could be further from the truth. This lie is just like the story Henry Drummond in the world-renowned play of *Inherit the Wind*.

Whenever somebody is telling a lie, look behind the paint and if it is a lie, then call it out for what it really is. And the lie is that the senate was never corrupted by any state legislator or state legislatures.

It is easier to plan corruption by one individual than a group of individuals. There only has been ten (10) rumored sources of corruption in the pre-direct election of senators while in the post-direct election of senators, we have seen multiple cases of corruption.

"How often, in connection with senatorial elections, resort has been to bribery or to corrupt pledge of office, it is impossible to determine. This much is certain, that in not less than seven States, during the past… years, charges of corruption have been put forward with evidence to make them a national scandal." (George Haynes, *The Election of Senators, 51*).

I.	1857. Simon Cameron (Pa); Certain members of the Pennsylvania Legislature protested against the seating of Cameron on the charge, among others, that his election had been procured "by corrupt and unlawful means." **The senate committee, to which these charges were referred, reported that the allegation was entirely too vague and indefinite to justify the recommendation of an investigation by the Senate.**

II.	1872. S.C. Pomeroy (Kan.); The Senate committee reported that the charge of bribery and corruption "totally failed to be sustained by any competent proof. **No further action was taken.**

III.   1872. Powell Clayton (Ark.); The committee recommended **the adoption of a resolution that the charges were not sustained.** This was agreed to. A minority report contended that there was evidence that Clayton had secured votes by the gift of money and of lucrative offices.

IV.   1873. Alexander Caldwell (Ark.); The committee recommended to the effect that Caldwell "was not duly and legally elected." **Caldwell resigned his seat.**

V.   1875. George E. Spencer (Ala.); The committee found the charges "not proven" **The Senate took no further action.**

VI.   1877. LaFayette Grover (Ore.); The committee reported that the evidence taken **did not sustain any of the charges.**

VII. 1879. John J. Ingalls. (Kan.); Both the majority and minority reports exonerated Ingalls from personal complicity in bribery; but it was held to be proved that corrupt means "were made use of both by those favoring and by those opposing his election." **The Senate took no further action…**

VIII. 1886. Henry B. Payne (Ohio.); By a vote of 44 to 17 the Senate decided to make no further investigation of the charges against Payne.

IX. 1898. M.A. Hanna (Ohio.); A majority of the committee reported that there was no evidence that Hanna was elected by Bribery; or that he authorized his agents to use corrupt means, or that he had personal knowledge of the alleged bribery. **The Senate took no further action.**

X. 1899. W.A. Clark. (Mont.); The committee reported that Clark "was not legally elected," since of his apparent majority of fifteen, more than eight votes had been obtained through illegal and corrupt practices. **Clark resigned his seat**, after making a strong speech in his own defense, (May 15, 1900).

(George Haynes, The Election of Senators, 53-56).

Out of ten, only two situations resulted of senatorial resignations with alleged corruption reports. Out of these ten cases, there were the subject and attention that needed to remain in the eyes of each of the sovereign State. Why did the national Senate had to interfere in investigating? To waste improper federal government funds in trying to investigative senate appointment elections is that long road we have been taking on this rogue and arrogance of an abusive power. It is the state legislature that needs to investigate these corruption matters. They are the ones that had this authority if they should keep or replace their senate delegation, not the federal government. To make recommendations on one State's way to conduct business, is to open a Pandora's Box for not needed increased power of the federal government.

In the first place, the Senate finds no warrant for investigating and no possibility of punishing corrupt practices in a state legislature by or [on] behalf of a candidate who does not secure enough votes of a can-election." (George Haynes, *The Election of Senators, 57)*.

It was the federal government that began this nonsense of control that led to these potential scandals of "rumored" corruption. The 1866 act was nothing more but to further regulate the national Senate. This act was established just after a bloody and unnecessary conflict between the States and the federal government. The States in rebellion were once again admitted to the republic. The prosperity of life, liberty and the pursuit of happiness was returning once again to this American republic of sovereign States. But the anger of several members of the federal government had not disappeared. Therefore, the radical Republican control of the national Congress began institutionalizing control over the several States to control their ability to retain their sovereignty.

"That the Senate's refusal to follow up an investigation or to expel a member is not always the equivalent of giving a clean bill of moral health to the legislature or to the senators may be inferred from the outcome of the Payne case." (George Haynes, *The Election of Senators, 57)*.

There was no reason to instigate anything further with federal legislation to control the several States, especially with unconstitutional legislative matters. The issue of civil rights is a different matter and that remains to be constitutional.

Deadlocks and vacancies done by the individual and sovereign State are no business but the affected State. The denying of that State to send their representative delegation to the national Senate.

"As the end of a session of a state legislature approaches, the efforts to secure the election of a senator at all hazards become more and more desperate. "In vain, in vain, the all-consuming hour. Relentless falls." But, since 1890, in ten states the parting knell has struck for the legislatures, leaving fourteen seats in the Senate vacant." (George Haynes, *The Election of Senators, 59-60)*.

"How has the membership of the Senate been affected? In the case of Louisiana, by reason of the long term of the legislature, by reason of the long term of the legislature, it was possible to make the election at the next regular session before the seat actually became vacant."
(George Haynes, *The Election of Senators, 60)*.

"In three of the States, the alternative of a special session was chosen. In Kentucky, the legislature was in session nearly seven weeks. The deadlock again developed immediately, and lasted from week to week. For four days a quorum was prevented, but, at the last, Deboe, who had been nominated only five days before, was elected. In Oregon, the State had been too outraged by the fiasco made by the legislature at the time of the regular session to tolerate any dilatoriness, and an election was effected on the fourth day. In California, the special session lasted thirteen days." (George Haynes, *The Election of Senators, 61)*.

What these sessions cost the States either in money or in derangement of public affairs, it should be the concern and only the concern of that State. It is not the concern of other States or even the national government.

"As the session wears on, the animosities engendered in the deadlock cannot be laid aside when the joint assembly adjourns from day to day: they project themselves into the ordinary work of the lawmaking body; giving a party color to the most non-partisan measures, distorting the legislator's views of many of the state issues and preventing the straightforward carrying on of the normal work for the legislature. This interference may vary through wide degrees of seriousness.

"What these sessions cost the States either in money or in derangement of public affairs it is impossible to compute with accuracy." (George Haynes, *The Election of Senators, 61)*.

Almost plaintive is the resolution, adopted just before the taking of the twenty-second ballot in the joint assembly which had suffered sadly from these trials:

"WHEREAS, The duty of electing a United States senator, while of great importance, is not the sole and only duty of the Legislature, and there are many other matters and things of vital interest to the people to be considered and determined during the brief constitutional life of this body, and;

WHEREAS, There is apparently no reasonable ground for the belief that the pending senatorial contest will be ended within the short time and the tedious repetition of ballots brings the Legislature no nearer the desired consummation, therefore be it;

Resolved, By the Legislature of the State of Washington in convention assembled: That during the present sitting of this body and hereafter during the present session, when convened for the present purpose, the Legislature shall take two ballots—and thereupon dissolve the joint session and endeavor to do some other business of the State."
* January 20, 1903.

(George Haynes, *The Election of Senators, 66-67)*.

If the sovereign State of Washington cannot seem to get their act together to send their delegation to Washington City. Then it should not be the concern or problem of other several

States or even the federal congress, the national Senate. The business of the State does consist of the appointment of their senate delegation. As I stated before, appointing a Senator is just like voting for a legislation.

I have seen a state legislature endlessly debate to pass or not to pass for a legislative matter into law. Sometimes they would take weeks, months, and go into special sessions to vote for a legislation. It is no different and it should not be any different.

The senate delegation of Washington State did not achieve to arrive to the national Senate for attendance. Then their interests would not be served in that session, and they would have learned their lesson until the next session. We the States, are not going to punish other sovereign States with excessive regulations from the federal government just because of literally one bad apple.

"Congress set about the task of improving upon the work of the fathers by prescribing a system of regulation, intended to correct the abuses which had arisen in connection with senatorial elections. Experiences such as these, exceptional though they still are, have nevertheless become so frequent and widespread that in recent years they have given rise to a determined propaganda, which no longer contents itself with an attempt to correct obvious defects in the law by which Congress has regulated the election of senators, but which demands that these elections be placed directly in the hands of the people." (George Haynes, *The Election of Senators, 69-70)*.

Untrue statement in the beginning of this paragraph. Congress was set not to task of improving the works of the framers in dictating to correct any so-called abuses in how the several States ran their senatorial elections. If this were to be true, then Congress has the authority to delegate a system of regulatory procedures to correct the abuses of the Electoral College elections. This is a pursuit of not correcting the abuse but of sweeping it under the rug and creating more of a problem. They instigate a propaganda ideal stating that the federalism principles that our constitutional framers established is not working and therefore, wanting to change it by claiming that they want to place in the hands of the popular masses.

Putting an election of a senator in the hands of the people, which was never meant to happen, would open more of a Pandora Box of political corruption. A grandiose amount of corruption would lead the way to hurt this republic even more.

Not only corruption will arise, but dismay, despair and the thoughts of broken promises will be more out in the open. It will be ever worse than President Lincoln's broken promise of "Forty Acres and a Mule" promise.

The direct election of Senators will be able to make promises, but they will not be able to comply them, because it is not in their federalism nature of that bicameral system.

April 8, 1913 was the date that was the end of our American Republic of sovereign States. The beginning of the American Democratic of Dependent States. The establishment of the unprincipled Seventeenth Amendment. And in connection with the Sixteenth Amendment, two months before in 1913, was truly the last two nails into the American Republic's coffin.

But I feel the fight is far from over for the American people and I believe that we can regain their state powers if they put their faith, money, and influence in repealing this mess of these two unprincipled Amendments that are dismantling our American Republic of sovereign States.

We will get to the various cases of corruption and broken promises, post 17th Amendment era in the next chapter. I will show you the absolutely disregard to our federalism principles that brought the Seventeenth and brought nothing, in my personal and humble constitutional legal scholar mind, shame to America.

II.

"The Senate of the United States shall be composed of two Senators from each State, elected by the people thereof, for six years; and each Senator shall have one vote. The electors in each State shall have the qualifications requisite for electors of the several State Legislatures. When vacancies happen in the representation of any State in the Senate, the executive authority of such State shall issue writs of election to fill such vacancies: Provided, That the legislature of any State **"may"** empower the executive thereof to make temporary appointments until the people fill the vacancies by election as the legislature may direct. This Amendment shall not be so construed as to affect the election chosen before it becomes valid as part of the Constitution."

Seventeenth Amendment to the
United States Constitution

The once esteemed national upper house of the nation's Congress has reluctantly become a haven of autocratic masses that paved the way of a now democratic unity of dependent States, rather than a representative unity of sovereign States.

After the Seventeenth Amendment was unfortunately ratified by the several States, it paved the way for an uncontrollable new form of corruption and embarrassing actions by those members. The spectrum of our republic changed dramatically, socially, culturally, and politically. These senators are now being popularly elected, competing like cattle for the first prize at the County Fair. This was something our Founding Fathers were adamantly opposed to, and always stood by their initial decision of electing national Senators.

These anti-American constitutionally challenged and progressive-minded individual thinkers were trying to find a way to control the business way of life of a state. And they found it by attacking the very same institution that promoted the sanity of American federalism and individual state sovereignty. You must remember that these individuals were in control of the federal government, and they were the ones that just won an internal war between the States. Granted, this war was a war to bring an end to the horrible hard-labor institution known as slavery. But it was not meant to abolish State sovereignty. I have always stated that "slavery may have been abolished, but state sovereignty did not."

The very idea from the Constitutional Framers that supported the idea of federalism, never dream that the principle of state sovereignty would cease to exist in 1865. As I mentioned earlier, some members of the federal government, champions of the civil war, wanted to see a crushing defeat of state autonomy and a rising tribute to centralized autonomy. What more to have centralized autonomy than with the illusive form of populism.

During the 1787 constitutional convention, the debate for the electoral method of national senators was a talkative discussion and debate. There was a small but overwhelming minority of delegates wanting the source to be direct election.

"James Wilson, the sole advocate of direct election by the people, was prompt in his opposition. He insisted that if one branch of Congress should be chosen by the legislatures and the other by the people, the two would rest on different foundations, and that dissentions would arise between them. Moreover, he held that it was wrong to increase the weight of the state legislatures by making them the electors of the senators; he believed that all interference between the general and local governments should be obviated as much as possible." (George Haynes, *The Election of Senators, 100-102)*.

With all due respect to Mr. Wilson, but that was the entire point in having this type of bicameral system. In this a more perfect union of sovereign States, the theory in place can be achieved in the place of reality. That is what most of the Framers of the Constitution were trying to seek to keep these two different chambers separate from one another.

Different ideas can function better and achieve the main objective if that objective is to preserve and maintain the republic. One chamber is there to protect the rights of the people, and the other chamber is to protect the rights of the States. They both lead to protect the constitution for both the people as well as the several States.

There is a balance of power between these two legislative branches. One is not trying to show privilege to the other. Both must remain equal under law for their States and people.

I can honestly say that populism increases the political weight onto the national House of Representatives than the national Senate. Populism is also described as vanity. While the then-Senators being in the upper chamber happen to have less vanity. I am speaking in the pre-1913 era.

In the National Senate, the only one that you must impressed are the State Legislators via-the people. Appointing a Senator is very much like voting for a piece of legislation. It is both to show for the best interest of the State and its residents.

Of course, the man that wrote the principled document had strong words to describe the main objective of elections of senators.

"Madison insisted: "The Senate will seasonably interpose between impetuous counsels, and will guard the minority, who are placed above indigence, against the agrarian attempts of an ever-increasing class who labor under all the hardships of life and secretly sigh for a more equal distribution of its blessings." (George Haynes, *The Election of Senators, 9-10)*.

Madison and most of the constitutional framers knew how important was to have an independent bicameral systems in the national government. They are electorally different but, in the end, they are the same, fighting to preserve and maintain the republic of sovereign American States.

"In defending the Constitution before South Carolina convention, Pickney laid strong emphasis upon this point. The House of Representatives, he insisted, would be elected immediately by the people and would represent them and their personal rights individually; the Senate would be elected by the state legislatures and represent the States in their political capacity; and thus each branch would a form a proper and independent check upon the other, and the legislative power would be advantageously balanced." (George Haynes, *The Election of Senators, 12*).

Thomas Pickney, a great framer to our Constitution, along with James Madison knew how to establish and build this republic. He could not have explained it in better defining terms of how each branch had their representative form of representation.

Thus, in creating a unity of good spirit to come together for these branches with the same constitutionalist idea for this nation. And to maintain that same idea, both chambers would remain independent from one another to present a form of checks and balances.

When I mean to present a form of independent checks and balances, I do not mean to have House members start caning Senate members, i.e., the caning by Rep. Preston Brooks against Sen. Charles Sumner.

This was unfortunate event in our American republic way of life that we shall never be repeated. The national and state bicameral legislative system is the most unique in its respectful decorum known to the world. We can never allow ourselves to behave in how Rep. Preston Brooks behaved.

There will be disagreements among these members, but the sense of respect, decorum and decency must come first before debating the issues of the day. Our American republic of sovereign States was built on the idea to agree and disagree with the opinions from our citizens without the introduction of insults and/or violence.

In the case of Preston Brooks, there is a reason the national House of Representatives is known as the People's House. The people are being represented by their peers. It goes to say which assembly is the populist run-mob. The other chamber remains at ease with herself.

Now we have seen how the national senate behaves like they do in current day to day events. They went from a prestigious and respectful organization to simply behave like their peers from the other chamber. The upper chamber of the national Congress was never intended to behave like their esteemed colleagues from the lower chamber. This is what the Seventeenth Amendment did to the most prestigious institution; the world has ever seen. An institution to be elected by a sovereign structure, not by a sovereign substance. The state is their sovereign structure form of representation, not to be confused by the population masses that reside in that State.

* * *

Another unsuccessful attempt was made in 1826 by Rep. Storrs of New York but the proposal failed at first sight. Then in 1829, Rep. John C. Wright of Ohio made another unconstitutional attempt in 1829. This attempt consisted of the two senators but would have a term limit of four years, this 1829 attack also failed. Between 1850 to 1855, Congress tried to pass similar resolutions of direct popular elections of Senators, but they all failed. (George Haynes, *The Election of Senators, 100-102)*.

The idea of direct popular election of senators have always been floating around even before the civil war. But the progressive-minded individuals were pursuing another issue, with better moral and just purpose (slavery). So, this purpose of popular elections of senators died for a short period of time. If only these individuals would focus in realizing the true nature of the federal government after the civil war, state sovereignty would be an integral part of our American republic.

"The proposed measure is often urged as necessary in order to render the government of our great federal state more consistently democratic. Modern democracy in dogmatic, and impatient of inconsistencies. "What the people are authorized to do indirectly through the means of the ballot, they should be permitted to do directly through the medium;" "the people are intelligent enough to choose their governors;

why should they not elect United States senators also?" "an amendment giving the election of senators to the people is but a just tribute to the intelligence and integrity of the individual voter;"—such are the phrases in which this movement is often set forth. "Gratitude," said the French cynic, "is an exceptionally lively sense of favors to come." When, on the eve of an election, a senator's appreciation of and gratitude to the people, seeks expression in such sounding phrases, hard-hearted, or hard-headed, indeed, would be the voters who would fail to see, in the perspicacity which had discovered in them such eminent qualities, proof positive of statesmanlike ability clearly entitling the candidate to reelection for another term. More and more, American government has been democratized, in the sense of the voters taking power directly into their own hands." (George Haynes, *The Election of Senators, 215-216)*.

To create an illusion that the candidates for senate appointments by the state legislators curtailed political and special interest favors is a progressive lie filled with hatred towards our framer's principle on federalism. Promises and favors have always been the tactic and weapon for populist elections. Promises made to the public are interpreted as favors that would eventually lead to broken promises.

This is what the framers questioned and worried about having a bicameral system of both elected by the populist masses. You give too much popular influence on a legislator; it will lead to a broken and corrupt system. I will gladly give examples of corrupt examples that occurred while the people elected the national senators.

"The demand still grew in congressional debate for direct popular election for senators. Political parties began to add this idea unto their platforms. The argument grew so strong that on April 13, 1900, a resolution was introduced to the states to propose an amendment for direct popular election of senators. The vote ended to be 244 Yea, 15 Nay and 88 Not Voting. (George Haynes, *The Election of Senators, 112-113)*.

"This resolution came after the bribery and corruption scandal of Montana Senator William Clark. There were at least continuing fighters in the senate that believed in the constitutionally principled state represented senatorial chamber. Senator Chauncey Depew of New York blocked any measure in the Senate that consisted to an amendment that the qualifications of citizens were entitled to vote for United States senators.

(George Haynes, *The Election of Senators, 116)*.

The American people were not as fed up as much on the news being spewed against by the distinguished national senator from Montana. The people honestly had no choice but to go along with the (Republican)-progressive agenda of direct popular senatorial elections. The passage of the both the Sixteenth and Seventeenth Amendments were not so much a passage for "We the People", but "We the general government". These amendments are not

"A republic can survive without the need of political parties. It survives on principle and not of partisan."

truly a part of the Bill of Rights, regardless that they continually state that the 17th is a people's voice for representation. If the Seventeenth Amendment really wanted to be a voice for the residents of their residing State. Then these progressives would have instituted a German-style of upper house chamber where their Senator is proportionally elected by districts. But the Seventeenth Amendment remained as "Two Senators from each State, elected by direct popular vote".

Why come two senators represent the popular representation of a large State like California or New York or Pennsylvania? I can answer this question in one simple sentence. The national Senate was never supposed to have a constituency. But that is what happens when progressives in power do to the Constitution. They change it for special interests only, and never with founding principle.

The Seventeenth Amendment made a huge dent to our American principle and Constitution. There was truly no point in creating this

amendment because people were still being represented with or without going to vote for their senatorial delegation. As then-Governor Jeff Davis of Arkansas and then-senator once stated, ".... the legislature has no duty depending upon them but to cast their vote for the person the successful candidate by the state convention. This is equivalent to the election of the people. You see, this can happen in this state because the nominees of the Democratic party are considered elected, as our legislature consists of 135 members and only two are Republicans."
(George Haynes, *The Election of Senators, 138)*.

This scheme to make the national senate elected by the popular masses was orchestrated by the Republican-Progressive Party, at that time. The Democratic Party were the ones opposed to this attack on our federalism. Now the tables have turned and now it is the Democratic Party supportive of the idea of direct election of senators. While the Republican Party being the one that opened the Box of Pandora, are now against it. The reason I despise a two-party system. A two-party system that continuously resides within this republic.

A republic can survive without the need of political parties. It survives on principle and not of partisan. Any popular government seeking to present their proposal of the need to prevail with political parties is creating an illusion of governance. Once a republic is vested on partisanship, it is no longer a republic, but a united democracy.

Then Governor Jeff Davis of Arkansas was a staunch opponent of replacing the principled election of senators to a random new populist form of elections. Even though, the people do not have the opportunity to elect their senatorial delegation, they are indeed voting for their state legislature representation. For a state legislator voting for a legislation, it is the same equivalency in voting for a senator. The people in the end would approve of the legislator's voting record at every election of that person's term. An indirect election in a federalism republic like this is one is indeed a direct election.

"The progressives' main reason to attack the way the senatorial delegation is full of flimsy and emotional rants that have no basis in truth. They stated that the current method of electing senators was a relic and had become obsolete." (George Haynes, *The Election of Senators, 153)*.

This national senatorial system worked way before 1866 and way before 1913. The problem was not in the state legislatures or the senatorial delegation picks, it was the intrusion of the central government. If the central power would not have intruded with their rules and regulations about how each individual state elected their senator, then there would still be more trust among the legislator's constituents. How come there was no distrust before 1866? If there were, then the system would have changed long before 1866 or 1913.

"The framers of the constitution with careful deliberation had adopted a plan which placed the election of senators in a small body of picked men, selected for a responsible service by their fellow citizens." (George Haynes, *The Election of Senators, 213)*.

The American people did not see the wrath of the Seventeenth Amendment not till after its ratification. Even during the progressive, unflattering years of Woodrow Wilson, the rage of the said amendment did not begin to pursue its reign of terror. The beginning senators, being elected for the first time by the popular vote, were unsure of what was their representation. To me, the national senators did not gain any constituency. The senators do not have a constituency regardless of what the amendment states. Their constituency will always be the sovereign States.

Their real test was not the introduction of prohibition of liquor sales and production. The added amendment to prohibit liquor to the States was just a legislation to show the rogue and arrogant power of the national government in the Twentieth century.

The real test did finally come to lighten the halls of the national senate. With the proposal of a national female vote. Across the nation, both republican and democrat progressives were shouting for equal voting rights for the American citizen of the female gender. Believing in not having national vote for female citizens does not make you a sexist. It makes you a constitutionalist. The Fifteenth Amendment guaranteed the right to vote citizens regardless of race or color. The Fifteenth Amendment was much needed to be a national cause because the black American citizens were being denied their basic rights as Americans across the republic. The female citizens were never denied of their basic guaranteed rights under the Constitution. The suspected murdered, later acquitted Lizzie Borden is one example that her right to due process was never denied.

The sovereign States of Wyoming, Montana and Colorado were showing great moves in showing great strengths in the access to women's rights including voting. It is called grassroots to see one State be ahead of its time and in due time other several States would have followed suit.

A national law imposed onto the States, to a State that the female population did not want it applied is a rule of tyranny. But to the new era of national senators being voted by the popular vote, are seeing this as a national issue and forgetting the principles of federalism and state sovereignty.

The Nineteenth Amendment was passed in 1919 and fully ratified by the time of the 1920 general elections.

A new era has finally arrived in the American Republic of sovereign States. An era of unbelievable democratic proportions to destroy the way of federalism. Because of the initiation of the Seventeenth, we have now seen a new wave of populism. Trying to appease to the religious right and female vote to end the liquor sale and production in America and then the female right to vote.

We have entered not the era of the Roaring Twenties but the era of the Roaring general government arrogance. And it began with the newly formed national Senate.

New Jersey national senator Walter Edge saw the advantage in asking for federal funds for the war veteran residents residing in the Garden State. After 1920, we have seen the use of the national Senate to achieve the unimaginable but with the assistance of the Sixteenth Amendment, it was a dream that woke up to be a nightmare. Not only in the unprincipled enforcement of the Revenue department to enforce the Eighteenth Amendment/Volstead Act. Funding for a national department to enter sovereign States to arrest, prosecute and imprison is beyond unprincipled. Unprincipled in the sense of totalitarian protective custody, all in the name of liquor. This was also the beginning that the national government started to show privilege under law for whatever State that asked or requested federal assistance.

I would say that America gained a break from this united democratic front during the presidency of Calvin Coolidge. Coolidge, while governor of Massachusetts was a progressive-minded individual. But as he got to the presidency after the untimely death of President Warren Harding. President Calvin Coolidge respected the rules of federalism and the individual and sovereign powers of the several States as well as the national government.

"In 1927, the mighty Mississippi River flooded parts of many southern states. President Calvin Coolidge knew that if he would have gone down there to administer and examine the devastated areas caused by the river, he might have encouraged the American people to accept the idea of federal spending on disaster relief. Instead, he sent Commerce Secretary Herbert Hoover. This of course triggered resentment among many members of Congress including the southern Senator of Arkansas, Thaddeus Caraway. He issued a statement against the president by saying, "I venture to say that if a similar disaster had affected New England, the president would have had no hesitation in calling an extra session." Just as the senator predicted, a flood swept across Coolidge's native Vermont. And did Coolidge visit his native land? The answer is no. Vermont and Arkansas received no federal intervention and they recovered on their own." (Calvin Coolidge and the Moral Case for

Economy, Amity Shlaes, author of Coolidge, Imprimis, a publication of Hillsdale College, February 2013, Vol., 42, Number 2).

This should inspire all people in public office, including members of the federal government, the national senators. The central government should not be beholden to any citizen of any sovereign State on behalf of the national senate or the chief executive. If they need to be beholden, then let them reach out to their perspective state government officials and national representative, but not to the national senators. Sadly, we have seen a different tune come to play where the senators have pleaded to the central power for federal intervention and aid. Later I shall continue to show you how national senators manage to steal the coffers of the national treasury from other States to pay for their own State's problems. The out-of-control spending and taxation policies have skyrocketed, thanks to the work of the unprincipled Seventeenth Amendment.

* * *

And here comes the wave of corruption that erupted in the national Senate. The progressive-minded individuals that concocted with the idea of popular elections of a senator. We only saw ten "alleged" corruption cases, prior to 1913. After 1913, we saw more alleged cases explode and the only solution was to disgrace the affected individual and expel him from the national senate. I will discuss the first two cases that were brought onto the high court and it was shameful. It was shameful that the progressives, from both political parties got their way to curtail their special interests first over the constitutional interests of the constitutional framers.

Prior to the Pennsylvania senate election of 1926, there was a contested senate election in 1918 in Michigan. Truman Handy Newberry was the republican candidate for the open senate seat in the Great Lakes State.

"This case concerned the Michigan Senate election of 1918 in which Republican Truman H. Newberry had run against Democrat Henry Ford, the manufacturer. Newberry had won the election, but the Senate refused to seat him on the ground that his primary expenses had been too large, as defined by the Corrupt Practices Act of 1910." (The Contested Senate Election of William Scott Vare, Samuel J. Astorino, 1961, 195).

"Newberry appealed to the Supreme Court which, on May 2, 1921, declared the Act of 1910 null and void because the Constitution did not give Congress the authority to regulate [primary] campaigns for nomination to federal office." (The Contested Senate Election of William Scott Vare, Samuel J. Astorino, 1961, 195).

This is what we resorted to, to truly beholden to the national Congress to dictate national directives onto the sovereign States. Especially national directives that remain lawless filled with loopholes. The ones that suffer with ridicule are the accused but truly the ones that must suffer are the accusers. The accusers have more ignorance and arrogance than the framers of the Seventeenth Amendment.

"The apathy or ignorance of the voter is more to be feared than the corruption of the voter." (The Vanishing Rights of the States: A Discussion of the Right of the Senate to Nullify the Action of a Sovereign State in the Selection of its Representatives in the Senate, James M. Beck, L.L.D; New York George H. Doran Company, 1926, 127).

The progressives that were in control of the general government knew quite well how to control the voter. They spring lies onto the public with no regard to the actual law. They make it appear that the real crook is the political candidate is the real crook. Denying the interests of the voter that elected this person to the office.

Why did Congress saw fit not to regulate primary elections? I cannot answer these questions because I am not the author or framer to the 1910 Corrupt Practices Act. But I can honestly say that the politicians in the federal government never think things through because of their arrogance. They only think to increase their power to whatever means necessary. Or honestly say that they imagined the high court would rule in their favor to justify their unconstitutionality.

Truman H. Newberry obtained electoral victory to be sat in the national senate to represent Michigan. Despite the corrupt allegations that were spewed during that election. The Constitution triumphed over gossipy rumors.

Of course, the allegations of corrupt activities during senate elections did not end in 1921, and it drags on for populist media attention.
I am going to put this question out there, to discuss the next and next alleged corruption case of a national senate election. "Why should be newsworthy of a corrupt allegation of a senate election from one sovereign State to be the concern of the other several sovereign States?"

To answer bluntly. It should not be the concern of anybody but the affected sovereign State if they so choose to act against that individual. This defeats the purpose of federalism and the very idea of state sovereignty. But to the individuals that perpetrated to write and finalize the Seventeenth Amendment, as well as the Sixteenth Amendment had no regard for the constitutional principle invoked in 1787.

The American Republic has always looked up to the Keystone State to remain true to their constitutional principles. Since it was a city within that state that began its work to build this American republic of sovereign States.

But we saw dangers of this new change to the beloved City of Brotherly Love in where Independence Hall.

The sovereign State of Pennsylvania had a senate election opened in 1926 and so the primary contention begins. We are here to discuss the Republican primary election that led to the winner of that primary race that later won the general election, the senate-elect winner, William Scott Vare. In the Republican party primary, there were three candidates: William S. Vare that won with 41.2 percent of the vote; George S. Pepper, incumbent, that obtained a vote of 35.5 percent; and Gifford Pinchot, Governor, that obtained a vote of 23.3 percent.

The incumbent candidate, Senator George S. Pepper, began his career as a progressive-minded individual but later it appeared to change his views to align himself with the current administration in power. Once an unprincipled progressive, always an unprincipled progressive. Then comes the Governor of Pennsylvania Gifford Pinchot, the other candidate.

"In 1922 all three groups were set back when Gifford Pinchot, the renowned progressive and bitter foe of bossism and corruption, captured the gubernatorial chair with his "Square Deal" campaign." (The Contested Senate Election of William Scott Vare, Samuel J. Astorino, 1961, 195).

In other terms, Governor Pinchot was the so-called Republican (reform) Party candidate trying to win over the populist vote on his alleged anti-corruption campaign. Pinchot was to be so untouchable and anti-corrupt that he came third in the primary race. A candidate who presents himself to be the incorruptible candidate, is indeed corruptible. For that reason, I believe that candidate Pinchot came in third and lost.

The people can be bamboozled by a smooth, populist candidate. These populist candidates do not deserve to have a representation or following. But they can smell the horse manure coming out that candidate's mouth, and I believe is what they saw out of Pinchot.

Candidate William S. Vare arrived at the primary race in first place and won to go ahead onto the general election. Candidate Vare went on to challenge William B. Wilson, a Democrat and former Secretary of Labor to Woodrow Wilson. William Vare received 41.2 percent of the vote against 35.5 percent of William Wilson's vote, establishing Mr. William S. Vare to be the next senator of the great sovereign Commonwealth of Pennsylvania.

"Rumors and complaints of fraudulent voting procedures had sprung up even before the May primary, and so loud, so persistent, and convincing were they that the United States Senate decided to launch an investigation into the matter. On May 17 it adopted a resolution (S.R. 195) introduced by James A. Reed, Democrat of Missouri, creating a special committee to look into the primary expenses of Vare in Pennsylvania and Frank L. Smith of Illinois. Reed was chosen to head the committee, and throughout the summer and fall campaigning special agents invaded to gather evidence. On

December 22, Reed issued the committee's report on expenditures for both the primary and regular elections, as follows:

Vare-Beidleman...................... $788,934
Pepper-Fisher..................... $1,804, 979
Pinchot............................. $187,029
Wilson............................... $10, 088

(The Contested Senate Election of William Scott Vare,
Samuel J. Astorino, 1961, 191).

"Until now no responsible official of the Commonwealth had made a formal statement against Vare, but on January 10, 1927, Governor Pinchot, following customary procedure, submitted the usual letter of certification of the Senate race to President Coolidge and literally dropped a bombshell of proceedings. Pinchot stated that Vare had been elected on the face of the returns, but was not "duly chosen" because "his nomination was partly bought and partly stolen." Pinchot, who held himself to be the symbol of the struggle against dishonest election practices in Pennsylvania, felt that the election of 1926 merely served to confirm his view that bossism should be ruthlessly stamped out. The letter became one of the main arguments against seating Vare, and in the hands of such a fellow-progressive as Senator George Norris of Nebraska, it was indisputable evidence that Vare had won by deceit." (The Contested Senate Election of William Scott Vare, Samuel J. Astorino, 1961, 192).

Rumors lead to gossip that leads to unfair discredit towards the affected man. Pinchot and candidates like him that know deep down that they are unpopular with the masses and will resort to anything to discredit his opponent. A scorned political candidate feels the scorn and wants you to feel this way, even if it's at the expense of somebody else.

I do not see anything wrong with the expenses of these candidates. If the expenses should be questioned, it would have been the incumbent. Senator Pepper had over one million dollars in campaign donations.

"The Mellons replied by supporting Pepper and John S. Fisher." (The Contested Senate Election of William Scott Vare, Samuel J. Astorino, 1961, 190).

"It was a Tammany Congressman who once jocosely asked a great and noble democratic President— "what is the Constitution between friends?" The historic anecdote failed to tell us what Grover Cleveland's reply was. He was a Democrat of the old school and believed no party advantage could possibly justify an invasion of the Constitution. The joke became historic, and it was not as silly as it seemed." (The Vanishing Rights of the States: A Discussion of the Right of the Senate to Nullify the Action of a Sovereign State in the Selection of its Representatives in the Senate, James M. Beck, L.L.D; New York George H. Doran Company, 1926, 18).

"While the Constitution may, and generally does, survive "between friends," a more serious danger is presented, when the question arises as to the strength of its guarantees between political friends and enemies." (The Vanishing Rights of the States: A Discussion of the Right of the Senate to Nullify the Action of a Sovereign State in the Selection of its Representatives in the Senate, James M. Beck, L.L.D; New York George H. Doran Company, 1926, 18-19.).

I believe the anecdote is true but as we do not know President Cleveland's response. I can rest assured that it was a very distinguished and noble response. A response with no sense of partisanship and a strong sense of principle and American ethical values.

The Constitution cannot be the support and rely on any kind friendships, political friendships, plain enemies, or political enemies. The Constitution must remain neutral in the eyes of the law and towards all citizens and sovereign States. That is how a republic must remain intact when there is unprincipled compromise. Once the Constitution is compromised with friendship, it no longer represents equality, but represents privilege.

The Seventeenth Amendment brought that to the national senate. It brought privilege of the rule of law to one senator but presumed guilt and shamefulness to the other.

The Mellon family from New York threw their support towards the incumbent. A powerful New York family with a portfolio in the financial market of Wall Street. Also, a member of that family was a cabinet member in Washington City. If any rumors need to afloat somewhere, then it should have landed in the Senator Pepper's financial records. But since this person lost the race, the accuser did not seek to question him but to question the winner's integrity, which he only received around $788,934 in donations should not be welcomed in any investigative committee.

"I do not question the power of the Reed Committee to make the investigation nor the high motives which prompted its members to pursue their investigations." (The Vanishing Rights of the States: A Discussion of the Right of the Senate to Nullify the Action of a Sovereign State in the Selection of its Representatives in the Senate, James M. Beck, L.L.D; New York George H. Doran Company, 1926, 16.).

"While the author prefers to discuss this matter independently of any existing party divisions, he cannot refrain from expressing his surprise that distinguished members of the Democratic Party, whose historic policy has been that of States' rights, should expressed themselves as in favor of a course of action, which would be the destruction of the most vital and basic of these rights." (The Vanishing Rights of the States: A Discussion of the Right of the Senate to Nullify the Action of a Sovereign State in the Selection of its Representatives in the Senate, James M. Beck, L.L.D; New York George H. Doran Company, 1926, 26.).

This is the problem in where partisan politics interferes with in of the Constitution. This two-party system that plagues our republic has never stood for federalism. There have been a few members of the national senate, from both parties that stood for federalism and for their sovereign State. Most of the members of the national government stood to protect the realm of centralization over sovereignty of their State.

It is the idea of party politics that is killing this republic. We need to find the integrity and sovereign of the individual to restore the republic, and not the politics or party of it. The Democratic Party once claim to stand for the idea of States' rights for the personal and impractical indulgences of life. Now they stand on nothing but to obtain full power with no regards to the electorate. The Republican Party was never for the idea of states' rights. Now they stand on this on a populist illusion platform. In the end, no party has ever stood for the principle that was bestowed in the national Senate. No political party in this American republic has ever guarded for the protection of States' rights onto their sovereignty of the State.

In this case of alleged corrupt allegation, the Chairman that resided in the investigative committee was a Democrat, Senator James Reed of Missouri. A Republican senator made his interest known in forming his own investigative query was Senator George Norris of Nebraska. When bipartisanship and political partisanship takes over constitutional principles, the end of the republic is near.

I do question anything coming out of the national government of their branches. That after Governor Pinchot came out with this alleged report of corruption against the Senator-elect Vare. Then other senators from other States decided to jump in the band wagon and began their own inquiries, all at the national level. Those national inquiries have a price tag on it, and it's the price tag of other States investigating a sovereign State. When populism becomes illusive, other people's money becomes no option for restraint.

"If this be so, the sovereign States do not themselves select their representatives in the Senate. They merely *nominate* them, and the ultimate judge is the Senate itself. This was the very method of selecting Senators which the Constitutional Convention rejected, as will be hereafter shown."

"Thus no doctrine would have surprised the framers of the Constitution more than this assumption. Indeed, it is safe to say that the Constitution of the United States would never have been adopted if its framers had conceived as a possibility any such power in the Senate. *If such a power shall be recognized, then the greatest if the rights of the States will have vanished." (emphasis added)* (The Vanishing Rights of the States: A Discussion of the Right of the Senate to Nullify the Action of a Sovereign State in the Selection of its Representatives in the Senate, James M. Beck, L.L.D; New York George H. Doran Company, 1926, 17.).

The framers never wanted this upper chamber to be popularly elected as the lower chamber. It was common sense to understand the framers' mind as the created this republic. The Solicitor General in defense of Senator Vare's allegation of corruption case knew and explains quite clear the framers frame of mind in designing the national senate.

"It seems to be generally assumed, and was assumed in the resolution offered by Senator LaFollete in the closing days of the last session of Congress, that the Senate has absolute power to expel any member whom it thinks unworthy of membership in that body, even though the people of the State, which accredited the member as its representative, are of a different opinion." (The Vanishing Rights of the States: A Discussion of the Right of the Senate to Nullify the Action of a Sovereign State in the Selection of its Representatives in the Senate, James M. Beck, L.L.D; New York George H. Doran Company, 1926, 24.).

"The Senate was created by the Constitution to preserve the rights and prestige of the States. The members of the House of Representatives more truly represented the new force which was then coming into existence, namely, the peoples of the States. The Senate, however, was intended to represent the States as political entities. To preserve the rights of the States, great and exceptional powers were given to the Senate. No law could be passed without the consent of the Senate. No important appointment to public office could be made without its consent. No treaty could have any efficacy unless two-thirds of the Senate concurred. No war could be declared unless the Senate so voted."

(The Vanishing Rights of the States: A Discussion of the Right of the Senate to Nullify the Action of a Sovereign State in the Selection of its Representatives in the Senate, James M. Beck, L.L.D; New York George H. Doran Company, 1926, 24-25.).

There is no doubt in my mind and in the hearts and minds of every single American, intellectual or not, to believe that the national senate represents the hearts and minds of the several States. The representation of the Senate which lies within its members to represent their State are there to maintain control of federal government influence and abuses against their State. The stature of the senate would not change regardless of how they are selected. With the inception of the Seventeenth Amendment, uncontrollable allowances have been given to the new national senators with no restraint. The representation drastically changed from a representative entity to a populist entity.

The powers that James M. Beck describes are the normal powers defined by the framers. Nowhere in the constituting of the formation of the national senate, it described that they have an absolute power to expel any members from service just because of allegations of rumors of corruption regarding their campaigns.

The arrogance of the federal government and of its branches never ceases me to amaze me to what lengths they will go to undermine the State's sovereignty and uplift their power.

Especially the rogue and arrogant progressive senator from Wisconsin, Robert LaFollete, that were one of the culprits that supported the birth of federal direct taxation and the uncouth direct popular election of senators.

"That the Senate has absolute power to expel any member whom it thinks unworthy of membership in that body,"

The sheer and utmost arrogance and betrayal to federalism. Also, a betrayal to the sovereign powers of the State of Pennsylvania.

"The sole question, therefore, is whether these States had the right to make such selections, or whether the Senate of the United States has the right to sit in judgment upon their deliberate voice." (The Vanishing Rights of the States: A Discussion of the Right of the Senate to Nullify the Action of a Sovereign State in the Selection of its Representatives in the Senate, James M. Beck, L.L.D; New York George H. Doran Company, 1926., 17).

In how this American republic was solely established, the question and answer are very clear. The States have always had a major responsibility in selecting their senatorial delegation. Whether it was through the state legislature or by direct popular elections. It is their retained right to manage their issues by themselves. The national Congress shares no inch of that responsibility to mettle in national senator selections. Or to that matter, the national Congress cannot simply expel a member of that institution simply of rumored corrupt allegations of their elections or previously appointments.

"We are, however, only concerned with the fundamental question of the power to nullify the action of a Sovereign State. It goes to the very foundation of constitutional government."

(The Vanishing Rights of the States: A Discussion of the Right of the Senate to Nullify the Action of a Sovereign State in the Selection of its Representatives in the Senate, James M. Beck, L.L.D; New York George H. Doran Company, 1926, 28.).

We are here to study and find out who has the legal authority to expel a member of the national senate and the reasons behind the expulsion. The respective sovereign State or the federal government's branch of the national Senate?

"Could the Senate judge primary elections? Did it have jurisdiction over a member-elect?"

(The Contested Senate Election of William Scott Vare, Samuel J. Astorino, 1961, 195).

"Then follows a very significant paragraph of Section 5:

Each House may determine the rules of its proceedings, punish its members for disorderly behavior, and, with the concurrence of two thirds, expel a member.

"It is very significant that the power of expulsion is dealt with in a different paragraph from the power given to the Senate and the House in the preceding paragraph, to determine whether one, who claims to have been elected, has in fact been elected, and if so, whether he possesses the "qualifications" which are prescribed in the Constitution. The two powers are distinct, and this is not merely indicated by the fact that they are dealt with in separate paragraphs, but by the even more significant fact that, while the question of an election and of the possession of the constitutional qualifications may be determined by a majority vote, the right to expel a member who has been given his seat requires a two-thirds vote." (The Vanishing Rights of the States: A Discussion of the Right of the Senate to Nullify the Action of a Sovereign State in the Selection of its Representatives in the Senate, page James M. Beck, L.L.D; New York George H. Doran Company, 1926, 49-50.).

"The scope and extent of the right to expulsion has been little discussed and rarely defined, for the reason that few attempts have ever been made to exercise this power." (The Vanishing Rights of the States: A Discussion of the Right of the Senate to Nullify the Action of a Sovereign State in the Selection of its Representatives in the Senate, James M. Beck, L.L.D; New York George H. Doran Company, 1926, 50.).

"In my judgment, the power of expulsion refers to some act of a senator *during his membership of the Senate*, and the act must have some reference to the discipline of the Senate. This is indicated by the words "punish its members for disorderly behavior." If a member persistently violated the rules of the Senate, and that body could no longer effectively function because of his deliberate interference with its labors, then the Senate, if it is to continue to exist, must have the power to punish the member for "disorderly behavior." (The Vanishing Rights of the States: A

Discussion of the Right of the Senate to Nullify the Action of a Sovereign State in the Selection of its Representatives in the Senate, James M. Beck, L.L.D; New York George H. Doran Company, 1926, 50.).

The rules of both Houses of Congress have been set since its inception in 1787. The rules for expulsion for the Houses in Congress and for the States have been set.

In my constitutional judgment regarding the expulsion of a Senate member is clearly defined for the roles of the national Senate. I must agree with James M. Beck's statement above stating that "the right of expulsion has been little discussed." It has been little discussed because this is the first time in our republic's existence where we have truly seen the national government's upper legislative branch behave in such a rudely and populist manner.

I must disagree with Mr. Beck's statement "and rarely defined." The definition is quite clear to the entities' power of expulsion. The disorderly behavior language in Section V does not need further defining by legal scholars. If a member of any of the national Houses of Congress acts in behavior not suitable while the Senate is in assembly. Then by a vote of two-thirds of that body has the right to expel that member.

Campaign finance reform laws and election laws are not and should never be an issue to be discussed, debated, and voted on in the national government, let alone in the national Senate. Election laws and procedures are designed to be legislated and regulated by each sovereign State.

"It may be—but I do not concede it—that if a Senator during the period of his service, is proved to have been guilty of some crime, he can be expelled, even though the crime has no relation to the discipline of the Senate. It is, however, equally clear, that the act which would justify his expulsion, must have taken place since his election. What he did prior to his election and the qualification has been passed upon by the people of his State. In a political sense, it is *res adjudicata*. A candidate for the Senate might have been guilty of embezzlement before his election, but the right of the people of that State to send an embezzler to the Senate, if it sees fit, is clear. Such decision is the sole right of the State. It must not be supposed that the general grant of power to each branch of Congress to determine the "qualifications" of its members gives unlimited discretion in determining the question of membership in the body. The general language which the Constitution uses must be read in connection with the entire instrument and, thus read, it is unreasonable that the power to judge of the "qualifications" of its own members was, or is, intended to destroy the rights of the States to select their own representatives in Congress." (The Vanishing Rights of the States: A Discussion of the Right of the Senate to Nullify the Action of a Sovereign State in the Selection of its Representatives in the Senate, , James M. Beck, L.L.D; New York George H. Doran Company, 1926, 50-51.).

If the so desired State or its people want to send a thief to Washington, it is their choice. A man of honest means is more likely to be dishonest as he enters the Halls of the Senate and settles down. The reputation of a man before he enters the national Senate should not be an issue of criminal inquiries and further convictions. To bring investigative inquiries of a primary election or general election to discuss the campaign donations, expenditures, or any type of malfeasance towards that member should be handled at each own state's discretion.

The State, or the people, respectively are the ones who decide how to treat the expulsion of their senator in these matters.

So, the question now remains, does the Senate have the jurisdictional authority over Primary elections upon its member-elect? The answer is a no, and the high court has affirmed that prior to the Pennsylvania senate election of 1926.

As the Supreme Court in 1921 stated that Congress has no authority to regulate primary elections.

"If the Congress has not seen fit, under any power which it may have under the Seventeenth Amendment, to make a regulation in respect to primary contests, then the Senate has no power to expel a Senator-elect on the ground that he or his friends spent an excessive amount of money in the primary contests." (The Vanishing Rights of the

States: A Discussion of the Right of the Senate to Nullify the Action of a Sovereign State in the Selection of its Representatives in the Senate, James M. Beck, L.L.D; New York George H. Doran Company, 1926, 73.).

"It is a significant fact, although the Newberry decision was rendered on May 2, 1921, and a doubt was expressed by one Justice (McKenna) as to the possible existence of a legislative power to regulate primary contests under the Seventeenth Amendment, Congress has not passed any such law and, in the absence of any such law, it must be assumed that Congress preferred to observe the historic policy of the nation, which is to leave such questions to the exclusive regulation of the States. This was undoubtedly the historic policy of America at the time of the adoption of the Constitution. The wise framers of that great charter of government recognized that even as to elections conditions would naturally differ and that election laws would require adaptation to their local necessities." (The Vanishing Rights of the States: A Discussion of the Right of the Senate to Nullify the Action of a Sovereign State in the Selection of its Representatives in the Senate, page James M. Beck, L.L.D; New York George H. Doran Company, 1926, 74-75.).

"As to these, the Supreme Court has decided that no power was given to the Federal Government, and this conclusion seems to the author of this book to be clearly demonstrated by the very able opinion of Mr. Justice McReynolds in the Newberry case.

"If it be practically true that, under present conditions, a designated party candidate is necessary for an election—a preliminary thereto—nevertheless his selection is in no real sense part of the manner of holding the election. This does not depend upon the scheme by which candidates are put forward. Whether the candidate be offered through primary, or convention, or petition, or request of a few, or as a result of his own unsupported ambition, does not directly affect the manner of holding the election. Birth must precede, but it is no part of either funeral or apotheosis. Many things are prerequisites to elections or may affect their outcome—voters, education, means of transportation, health, public discussion, immigration, private animosities, even the face and figure of the candidate; but authority to regulate the manner in holding them gives no right to control any of these. It is settled, e.g., that the power to regulate interstate and foreign commerce does not reach whatever is essential thereto. Without agriculture, manufacturing, mining, etc., commerce could not exist; but this fact does not suffice to subject them to the control of Congress. Election of Senators by state legislatures presupposed selection of their members by the people; but it would hardly be argued that therefore Congress could regulate such selection. We cannot conclude that authority to control party primaries or conventions for designating candidates was bestowed on Congress by the grant of power to regulate the manner of holding elections. The fair intendment of the words does not extend so far; the framers of the Constitution did not ascribe to them any such meaning. Nor is this control necessary in order to effectuate the power expressly granted. On the other hand, its exercise would interfere with purely domestic affairs of the State, and infringe upon the liberties reserved to the people."

(The Vanishing Rights of the States: A Discussion of the Right of the Senate to Nullify the Action of a Sovereign State in the Selection of its Representatives in the Senate, James M. Beck, L.L.D; New York George H. Doran Company, 1926, 80-81.).

As far as any rules to reward or punish a Senator with this added amendment is of no consequence and has no set precedent. It has no precedent for the Senate to punish a senator for allegations during his primary election and even his general election.

This is what happens when the high court makes a ruling in favor of federalism and you have a few Americans ignorant to the news or precedence.

And when you have corrupt leaders, you will be misled into the false ignorance of that leader for the achievement to gain his trust for his own special interests. Ignorant leaders like the Governor of Pennsylvania, Gifford Pinchot,

Senator George Norris; Senator Ted Cruz, and Donald J. Trump, President.

"The apathy or ignorance of the voter is more to be feared than the corruption of the voter." (The Vanishing Rights of the States: A Discussion of the Right of the Senate to Nullify the Action of a Sovereign State in the Selection of its Representatives in the Senate, James M. Beck, L.L.D; New York George H. Doran Company, 1926, 27.).

The false ignorance of the leader is more to be feared than the corruption of the leader. This happens when there is a legal precedent already established. Then a scandal arises of false ignorant promises due to a political scorned official looking for populist sympathy. In trying to reach populist sympathy, they will look to reach legislative support to break the law and seek an unconstitutional precedent.

Sen. William S. Vare is the victim of political unconstitutional corruption witch hunt that led to his downfall, thanks to this unprincipled amendment. He was eventually removed from office regardless of judicial jurisprudence precedence. This is the first in American republic history in where the national senate invented new rules in how to expel a senatorial delegate with no regard to federalism. There was no regard to the interests of the sovereign State and its people. That is where the national government stood tall with rogue and arrogance to disavow the policy of federalism and institute the policy of centralized autocracy.

This will not be last of an issue of a disputed primary race. As the unprincipled Seventeenth Amendment triumphed with unconstitutional policy and against the sovereign and independent States and its people.

* * *

After this sad state of American republic affairs in where we unwillingly give in to the awful will of the national government. The national Senate today has become a servant to central autonomy rather than to individual autonomy. The Seventeenth Amendment continues to run wild to let national Senators interfere in other States' business. We have let the national Senators support, propose, and legislate agenda against the will of their and other member's sovereign States.

After the 1926 senate election in Pennsylvania in trying to fully investigate Senator Vare if he committed campaign fraud in his primary. America forgot its true principle in national Senate politics and powers. The true winner was of course William S. Vare. But when we get tangled in partisan and corrupt politics, we forgot our true constitutional principles. We also forgot that the high court cannot force Congress to regulate a primary election, and therefore, the Senate had no constitutional authority to expel this Senator.

Our ailing American Republic went from making our sovereign States' rights into a mockery and exercising unprincipled federal government regulations. After 1926, we have seen multiple Senate elections come close in their vote tabulations. That we have seen primary too-close-too-call races go into run-off elections and sometimes second run-off elections. I will give the best primary too-close-too-call elections example of this, because it involved, one of the most corrupt individuals ever to set foot into Washington City politics.

It involved future president, Lyndon Baines Johnson, when he decided to seek the open Senate seat left open in Texas by everybody's famous Texan Southern political son, W. Lee "Pappy" O'Daniel.

The Republican primary, at that time in Texas was simply non-existent because the Democratic Party had controlled of the Lone "Dixie-crat" Star State. So, who ever won the Texas Democratic Primary would win the general election. The candidates for that primary were then-U.S. Congressman Lyndon B. Johnson and Governor Coke R. Stevenson. The primary election received unnecessary national media attention because LBJ, a crazed populist maniac wanted that and got it.

Both candidates did national and state political TV ad spots trying to get the attention of the entire country. Therefore, I made this statement and will revise it when I discussed the 1926 Pennsylvania Senate election. "Why should it be newsworthy regarding a Senate election in one sovereign State to get national media attention into other sovereign States?

And so, came primary voting day in Texas. And it was a populist mad house in when Julius Caesar posted himself to run for Consul of the Roman Senate. The results came in and Lyndon Johnson received 33.73 percent of the vote and Coke Stevenson received 39.68 percent of the vote. Honestly, if we did not have this Seventeenth Amendment of direct election of senators, Governor Stevenson would have won the election. But because nobody "obtained" the majority vote, the election went to a run-off election and that is where the election got even dirtier, filled with populist promises from both candidates. Promising the federal treasury key to be sent to Texas for pork barrel spending.

On August 30, around 11:45 at night, the votes came back and with a strong victory towards for Governor Stevenson. The vote count was, Stevenson received 492, 481 and Johnson a 492,271. It was clear that Stevenson was going to be declared the winner, till certain boxes of ballots appeared out of nowhere in Jim Wells County, Texas. Two-hundred ballots came in for Johnson, while only two ballots were reported for Stevenson.

The endless legal battle began to see who the real winner of the Texas State Democratic Party was. Stevenson took this battle to the Supreme Court but in the end, failed to achieve a political victory or electoral victory. Associate Justice Hugo Black sat in judgment as a Circuit Judge in this case. He decided that Congress had no legal jurisdiction authority to interfere in a primary party race being held by a party and not the federal government.

Lyndon Baines Johnson was unfortunately certified to be the junior senator of Texas. My question is why Governor Stevenson didn't take his complaint to the national Senate and ordered that the junior senator be expelled for possible corrupt campaign fraud in his primary (1926 Pennsylvania senate election). The national Senate surely had plenty of precedence and evidence.

And there you have it, another unprincipled victory for the unscrupulous Seventeenth

Amendment. This amendment has given a clear precedence to avoid further possible and actual primary and/or general election campaign fraud. The people would rather keep wearing the same dirty underwear, rather than investigating why it is dirty and to change it to better their lives.

We went from a nation of scrupulous Senate leaders, to a nation of unscrupulous and arrogant Senate leaders. These leaders hide their corruption in the name of populism. The primary election of 1948, to me, in the modern Twentieth Century, we saw crooked politicians disavow the Constitution and the proper voting method of their office they sought to further implement their own special interests. In my constitutional scholar mind, it began in 1948, has not yet ended and it continues to this day.

I am not going to go into other specific races because I am not here to explain the fallacy that the Seventeenth Amendment has created with other corrupt Senate popular elections. But after 1948, almost every Senate election held in a sovereign State that has received plenty of national media attention, like in 1948, has resulted in some corrupt alleged source of political campaign corruption.

Many American progressive-minded thinking individuals have made conclusions that state legislatures of several States were corrupted by the individual being nominated for the senate position. Nothing could be further from the truth. Just because the people indirectly voted for their national senator, does not mean that corruption was rampant. The people directly voted for their state legislator for them to vote for the best man to represent their State. If by some chance that "best man" was a disappointment to the State and its people. Then the people will decide to vote out their legislator and put somebody in that did represent them better and their State.

That to me, was a direct election of a representative republic. It was a direct line that the framers insisted it remain that way to avoid lies, corruption and arrogance. But 1913 changed everything and America, unfortunately will never be the same. We went from an in-direct line of uncorruptible elections to a direct line of corruptible elections.

President Eisenhower proposed an unconstitutional national measure against the sovereign States entitled the Interstate Highway Act." As we all know that national infrastructure legislations are to be unconstitutional as stated by the Father of the Constitution, James Madison. This man should know the Constitution quite well since he wrote it, even the Commerce Clause was never meant for federal regulations. It was meant for state-on-state regulations with federal administration.

Prior to 1913, and basically prior to 1865, the national senators stood tall to represent their State with no intimidation from the federal government. The national senators of today, elected by popular election, fail to vote to represent their state and vote to represent the national government. It's simply tragic to see the members of the upper house of the national Congress, get intimidated by other members of Congress or the national executive branch to vote in favor of a monstrosity of a federal government directive. A directive that most of the times remains unconstitutional and against the sovereignty of the several States. They either neglect to represent their State against these directives, or they have been bought with federal funds for a special interest issue for their State, or for their campaign and themselves.

This nation was built to be an American republic of sovereign States, not an American Democratic of Dependent States.

With the stock market crash of 1929, many national senators worried about their elections than the rules of federalism. We understand that many Americans were suffering quite extensively with the era known as the Great Depression. What the American people were not aware and to this day are neglected to come to the facts is that the main cause of the stock market crash was the intervention and meddling of the national government. How come we expect the federal government to help us out of a depression, if it was the federal government that got us into a depression. With the government of Herbert Hoover, Republican, proposed progressive legislation, excessive taxation, corporate regulation that his predecessor rejected. There was a reason that his predecessor's presidential term was known as the Roaring Twenties. Wall Street and Main Street was booming economically, socially, with extreme less government regulation and taxation. President Coolidge's successor disavowed the great legacy that was bestowed and went back to the terrible legacy of Woodrow Wilson.

Enter FDR and continued the Wilson-Hoover legacy of a federal government's reign of economic terror. The national senators, instead of standing up for their sovereign State, sided with a rogue and arrogant federal government. senators like Huey Long of Louisiana; Claude Pepper of Florida; Robert LaFollete, Jr., of Wisconsin; George W. Norris of Nebraska; and many more that sided with the arrogant national government over their sovereign State. Then enter LBJ's shameful Great Society policies, not including the 1964 Civil Rights Act and 1965 Voting Rights Act. But the other policies of his not-so-Great Society that senators bowed down to accept federal funds in sovereign States that were already suffering from the 1935 New Deal programs. Then enter Ronald Reagan and a slight conservative but still Democrat-controlled Congress that switched gears in unconstitutional representation and spending. They shifted those funds from social programs to funding the State of New York; City of New York, a small, but busy and rich street known as Wall Street. In the 1980s, the national Senate shifted its gears from representing the slums of the republic to the rich of the republic.

Then of course, during the pretense of national security, the federal government has intimidated tremendously the national Senate. After the terrible attacks that occurred on September 11, 2001, we could have seen a decrease or resizing of the federal government. Quite the contrary, and most of the national Senate voted to increase the size of the federal government with the implementation of a new executive department, protective custody tactics and an advanced control of the Naturalization Clause of the Constitution. This was known as the USA Patriot Act. With a name like that, it was bound to get lots of senator sell-outs against their sovereign State and beholden to an extreme enlargement of the federal government. Only one national senator voted against this measure, Russell Feingold of Wisconsin. I am not sure what his motives were but at least he stood against the federal government.

Let me also address the education crisis that is currently happening to our republic. The education situation is an issue that shall reside to the several States.

The federal government has no authority, constitutionally or legally to pass any measure for education. Ever since, the Jimmy Carter years that established the Department of Education, we have seen federal funds go from school district to school district, unapportion and unrestrained, across this republic with no outrage from any national senator. The 2001 No Child Left Behind Act made this situation even worse. If you think the federal government creates literacy, you are mistaken, it creates illiteracy.

National infrastructure programs were never meant to be applied to each sovereign State. Especially at the funding demand of the federal government.

President James Madison knew that national spending on infrastructure across the States was unconstitutional. He vetoed an 1814 Public Works Bill that would have given a green light for national funding for roads, canals, and bridges. Madison stated that there was nothing in the Constitution that gave those enumerated powers to the federal government. Powers that allow the general government of the United States to act as the nation's toll administrator for the sovereign States.

> **It is the sovereign States that are superior to the national government.**

The postal service is a branch of the federal government but that never implied that federal union officials had the authority to fund and create roads across the several States. The postal service mobilizes across this republic, but the states supply the roads to inter-connect with one another. To be a more perfect union, States need to work together under the guidance of the Constitution. We the States, respectively cannot let the federal government take command, buy its allegiance, and let the States bow down to their totalitarian ways of governance.

The New Deal programs saw a boost of federal infrastructure spending across the sovereign States in astronomical funding numbers. Sovereign States of New York, New Jersey, Florida, Georgia, and many more are still paying for half of the electric power plant of the Hoover Damn. This dam gives federal electric power to California, Arizona, and Nevada. And yet, the rest of the nation are paying for this monstrosity of infrastructure.

The federal government has traded favors with national senators to vote a certain way against the will of their State to be beholden to them. LBJ did favors for various senators for them to vote to pass the 1964 Civil Rights Act for federal funding for their States. He made a deal with Nevada Senator Howard Cannon for his vote and the federal government would approve funds for an infrastructure bill that would benefit Nevada only at the expense of other States. Other sovereign States would foot for the bill while Nevada enjoys that luxury.

This is something that Senator John C. Calhoun always stood against that South Carolina should never accept funds at the expense of other States via-the federal government. Then because that state is now forever in debt and beholden to those states and the national government.

But with the creation of the Sixteenth Amendment and the establishment of the Seventeenth Amendment, favoritism and privilege began in our daily republic's way of life. Now we have seen an increase of favoritism politics play drastically in the national Senate. Especially for funds for national infrastructure and humanitarian funds.

National senators are competing for those funds, for special interest only. They want to make sure that their so-called constituency see that he is "Delivering for their *State*". But they are delivering with other people's/states' money. They are indeed being unscrupulous about it to obtain the vote and keep winning in every single direct election.

We cannot say that California, New York, Illinois, Pennsylvania, etc., have the biggest unscrupulous senatorial delegations. The disease of unscrupulousness has spread to every single of the fifty sovereign States.

California's delegations become unscrupulous when demanding and getting federal funds for their infrastructure. They just received four billion dollars in federal funds to build a bullet train from San Francisco to Los Angeles. What favors Senators Feinstein and Padilla sought to get those funds. I love both cities.

But there is a reason that every state, including California has a state legislature with a state budget and an executive branch to dictate these issues on the sovereignty level of California. They do not need the federal government to dictate these issues on to them. Same goes with Florida when they received twenty-five million dollars for funding for the Brightline bullet train that currently covers the South Florida portion of that State. The same question goes to Senators Rubio and Scott on the funding question of the Brightline railway. The same question goes to Illinois Senators Durbin and Kirk when they obtained funds for a bullet train from Springfield to Chicago.

The federal government was not originally established to spread the wealth across the States. The federal government was there to administer the States to work together with their own wealth to connect greatly and under the supervision of the Constitution. But the federal government made an alteration in this original establishment and now we are seeing that they have become a superior father to the sovereign States. It is the sovereign States that are superior to the national government.

The federal government is not the salvation army to the sovereign States. As I mentioned earlier, the best story in where the federal government's executive branch under Calvin Coolidge remained neutral in not showing privilege to one State and not the rest. While the non-esteemed national senator from Arkansas was too keen to maintain his special interest support for his own national attention persona towards his potential reelection campaign rather than to his sovereign State.

That has been the attitude of national senators, post-1913 in this modern-American republic era. Whenever there is a natural disaster, and with the unconstitutional creation of the FEMA (Federal Emergency Management Agency). We have seen more beggars on Capitol Hill, on the national Senate side than on the national House of Representatives side.

Whenever a Hurricane hits the Texan coast; Florida coast; South Eastern and North eastern seaboard; an earthquake or wildfires hit the Pacific region; tornadoes hit the Midwest; floods arise due of the Mississippi River. The flock of corrupt national senators extend their hands for federal government assistance with other people's funds.

In 1992, Florida was hit with a category five hurricane. Hurricane Andrew made a disastrous landfall to the South Florida region. The late Governor Lawton Chiles examined the situation and welcomed the federal government assistance of President George H.W. Bush. The national senate delegation at that time, were no different to the ones today after Hurricane Ian hit the western Florida coast in September 2022. Both national Senators Marco Rubio and Rick Scott pleaded with the federal Congress to give assistance to Florida. And there is the current Florida Governor, Ron DeSantis, who is just as unscrupulous as Florida's senate delegation. Here is a state official that praised one federal government administration and not the other federal government administration. He hides his hypocrisy and extends his hands like Oliver Twist, "Please sir, may I have some more?"

When a national disaster is about to hit in their sovereign State. The state officials and national senate delegates put aside their hypocrisy and extend for hand-outs. That is the hypocrisy of the Seventeenth Amendment. This is a norm that our framers never wanted for their republic. They are only hiding their hypocrisy for their special interest in getting popularly elected every term.

In 2013, sovereign State of New Jersey Governor Chris Christie gave a "big hug" to President Obama for unconstitutional natural relief aid assistance due because of Hurricane Sandy. It was a sad spectacle to see a state official and the national senate delegation from the Garden State bow down to the national government.

In 2005, after the federal infrastructure levees failed to be raised to protect the City of New Orleans. Hurricane Katrina made unspeakable damage to that beautiful city. Then came the state officials from that State, its city officials, and its national Senate delegation welcome with opened arms the federal government. A famous picture of President George W. Bush and the late Governor Kathleen Blanco.

In 2017, Texas was hit with a category four Hurricane. Hurricane Harvey hit that sovereign State. The national senate delegation of that State are more of a disgrace than the New York or New Jersey. National senator Ted Cruz gladly opened his arms and welcome President Donald Trump.

While President Trump showed privilege to the State of Texas. The federal territory of Puerto Rico was suffering the wrath of a hurricane. Trump denied to personally go and assist them. Puerto Rico has more of a right to get federal assistance and protection than Texas given that they are a federal protectorate.

There you have the ignorance of the American voter than the common sense of the voter. The ignorance of the national Senator is worse than the voter's ignorance. That type of ignorance is filled with arrogance. A sense of privilege that they believe are above the law.

When Hurricane Sandy hit the shores of New Jersey, Senator Marco Rubio; Senator Rand Paul; and Senator Ted Cruz voted against federal aid to the Garden State. But when Harvey hit Texas; Ian hit Florida; and tornadoes hit Kentucky, they are up, front and center in asking for federal aid. The arrogance fills in with hypocrisy.

I have stated this many times, as a constitutional scholar and historian, that the national Congress, specifically, the national Senate is not a chamber to be conjoined with privilege and favoritism. The popularly elected national Senate along with the congressional authority to tax and spend has given a sense of leeway and privilege to seek funds to expand their special interests and/or their small interests of their State. They seek these funds to please the masses, to keep them in power.

* * *

When we see national senators play the privilege game towards conglomerate companies to gain favoritism is a sight to awful to bear because you question their morals as well as their ethics.

The national Senate has truly lost all sense of principles. And gain all sense of privilege.

One example, I can offer to you that will begin a world of privilege and favoritism was national Senator Ralph O. Brewster, Republican from Maine.

During the Truman years, he was authorized to chair a select committee on Defense due to the beginning Cold War situation. Businessman and airplane extraordinaire Howard Hughes was bidding for air force federal defense contracts. He was also opening his own commercial airline known as Trans World Airlines.

We have seen in multiple reports that Senator Brewster became a loyal friend to Pan American Airways CEO and a lobbyist in Washington City by the name of Juan Trippe. You could say that the political and business relationship between Brewster and Trippe was the beginning of lobbying scandals to seek personal and privilege favors from national senators. Favors that have never once intended to be to help and assist their State but it was favors to assist them in their own special interests. It was to be known that Pan American Airways obtained those European, Latin American, and Oriental routes because on the recommendations of Senator Brewster. It is to be known that Brewster went to several countries that this airline obtained routes at the expense of Pan Am's CEO Mr. Juan Trippe.

This style of political and business shady relationship between a national senator from Maine between a world-renowned CEO of an airline company. I mean, what does a national senator from Maine have to do in the nation of Peru or Cuba? There is no lobster alliance to initiate with Cuba or Peru.

This brought the beginning of pure corruption within the national Senate and private companies and their lobbyists.

In the first chapter, I mentioned to you that there have been only ten recorded "alleged" corruption cases involved with the State Legislature. Ten cases that brought two resignations but no expulsions from the Senate. There was also no concrete evidence to prosecute the entire ten cases.

Well, I am going to show you that post-1913, there has been twelve and more recorded political corruption cases and they are even worse than the pre-1913 ten. These twelve and more are all products of corruption brought by the populist, unprincipled Seventeenth Amendment for special interests. That special interest is to expand their fundraising for their upcoming and upcoming elections.

Populism creates corruption, and corruption creates hypocrisy, and hypocrisy creates arrogance. The hypocrisy of a national senator is just as dangerous as the arrogance of a national senator.

1. Bob Menedez (NJ) – Bribery, conspiracy, mail fraud, 2015. **Awaiting trial and still the incumbent.** As he

awaits trial more evidence has turned up against his corrupt activities, 2022.

II. Ted Stevens (AK) – Corruption for receiving gifts and making false statements, 2008. Conviction overturned because of prosecutorial misconduct. **Lost his bid for re-election**, and died in a plane crash in 2010.

III. Kay Bailey Hutchinson (TX) – Tampering with government records as Texas State Treasurer, 1993. **Acquitted**.

IV. David Durenberger (MN) – Misuse of public funds, improper reimbursement for nights he spent at home, 1993. Pleaded guilty to five misdemeanors in exchange for dropped felony charges; **no jail time**.

V. Harrison Williams (NJ) – Bribery as a result of an F, 1924BI sting that famously became known as Abscamon [correction: ABSCAM], 1981. At trial, Williams was seen promising (on camera) to use his influence to help an

Arab sheik, who was in fact an FBI agent. **Williams resigned** from the Senate before he was expelled and spent 21 months in prison.

VI. Edward Gurney (FL) – Bribery and lying to a grand jury. **Acquitted in 1976 but did not seek re-election in 1974**.

VII. Burton Wheeler (MT) – Conflict of interest, 1924. Accepted attorney's fees to represent a client at an Interior Department hearing. **Acquitted**.

VIII. Truman Newberry (MI) – Campaign spending violations, 1919. Convicted in 1921. Conviction reversed by the Supreme Court. **Left the Senate in 1922**.

IX. John Hipple Mitchell (OR) – Accepting cash in exchange for helping expedite land claims, 1904. **Convicted**. He died while his case was on appeal.

X. Joseph Burton (KS) Bribery. Accused of accepting $2,500 from a securities firm and intervening in a mail fraud case, 1904. Convicted, and served five months in prison. **Resigned from the Senate in advance of expulsion**.

XI.   Charles Dietrich (NE) – Bribery, 1904. Acquitted in court and found innocent by the Senate.

XII.   John Smith (OH) – Treason for conspiring with former Vice President Aaron Burr, 1807. Charges dropped after Burr was acquitted. **Resigned in 1808 at the request of his home state legislature, after an effort to expel him came up one vote short in the Senate**.

(There have been 12 U.S. senators indicted while in office.

Here's a list; Terence Samuel,

The Washington Post, April 2, 2015).

This journalist is stat-ing relevant facts to national Senate corruption. But he is not stating the change in gears that the republic endured to the national Senate. The method of electing a national Senator made a powerful impact to the nation and to each sov-ereign State. In 1913, the method changed from state legislature elections to populist elections.

The reason that the method changed was of a progressive "false" campaign that there was corruption within every state legislature while electing their national senate delegation. The corruption was alleged because in ten possible cases. Only three Senators were charged of a crime, two resigned. The rest either remained to finish their terms or died.

He reports eight cases of corruption in post-1913 era. While he only reports four cases in pre-1913 era. Let's touch first the pre-1913 cases. In these four cases of corruption, two senators resigned and two held their seat. The national senator of Ohio, John Smith, resigned at the request of the state legislature. That decision is not just on one state legislature. That's a state legislature power among the several States that had that power. But each state legislature should have been left alone to handle their senatorial delegations as they see fit.

The other senator, Senator Charles Dietrich, was acquitted by a court and later acquitted by the national senate. Why wasn't he put on trial at the state legislature of Nebraska? If both a court of law and the national senate found him innocent of bribery charges, then there isn't much corruption charges in his case.

There you see the beginning arrogance of the federal government, disavowing the lawful and power actions of a state legislature to vindicate the power of the general government of the United States.

Senator Joseph Burton of Kansas was accused of bribery. He was convicted of those charges and served five months in prison. He resigned from the national Senate because he heard rumors of expulsion. Again, why there was no voice from the Kansas state legislature on the rumors of expulsion. Why are we so accepting to accept the will of the federal government and not from their state legislature?

Senator John H. Mitchell of Oregon was convicted of accepting cash in exchange of favors. But while his case was on appeal, he died in office. He never thought to resign, the national Senate never proposed expulsion towards him, and there is no mention of the Oregon state legislature in reigning in this scoundrel.

Have we forgotten the will of each sovereign State and not to be beholden to the federal government? This was the surely the beginning of the end of our American republic of sovereign States.

I am not sure what this journalist is trying to state with this list of corruption, but he must know the difference in times. I do not care what people, the state legislatures of Oregon; Kansas; Nebraska; and Ohio elect. If they commit a crime prior, during or after their senatorial term. The entity that should handle their criminal proceedings should be their State, not the federal government. Unless the federal government can prove that the crime suggested is a federal crime.

Let's turn to Senator Truman Newberry of Michigan and his corrupt case brought against him in 1919. He was convicted but the Supreme Court reversed his conviction due because Congress does not have the authority to regulate primary elections. This case was the first case of an "alleged" corruption, six years after the passage of the Seventeenth Amendment. The federal court gladly sided with the sovereign State and not the federal government.

It is quite strange that this New York Times journalist, did not mention the "alleged" corruption case of William Scott Vare? But because there was a primary precedence with the Newberry case. Then this case is somewhat irrelevant in his mind. It is not irrelevant in mind, because the Vare case shows the true arrogance of the federal government against the several States. They denied the right for Pennsylvania voters decide the fate of William S. Vare and decided for themselves.

I am strongly against the direct popular election of senators, but when the national government takes away that voting right away from the State, respectively the people, it literally defeats the purpose of the Seventeenth Amendment.

Nobody has brought up a suit of corruption during a general election case, so therefore the argument remains open for debate. But I humbly believe and assume that Congress also does not have the power to regulate a general election, given that it is also a State electoral issue.

Now let's discuss the eight corruption cases, post-1913. Let's take first the case of Senator Kay Bailey Hutchinson. She was accused with tampering with state government records while she was Texas State Treasurer. This happened way before she ran for the senate seat against Bob Krueger. "A candidate for the Senate might have been guilty of embezzlement before his election, but the right of the people of that State to send an embezzler to the Senate, if it sees fit, is clear. Such decision is the sole right of the State." (Beck, *The Vanishing Rights of the States*.) Hutchinson was indicted during a time that she was not even a member of the national Senate. The issue with this journalist is that he is writing with emotions instead of with the law and Constitution. It is of no business of another State or to bring attention of the national Senate on an individual that was clearly elected by either the state legislature or respectively, the people.

The arrogance of the national Senate, because of the populist backing at every election has become ever more rogue and arrogant than the days of Montana Senator William Clark. According to this journalist's report, only one Senator resigned, while seven did not resigned, and one is still holding his seat. The Senator that resigned was Senator Harrison Williams of New Jersey. He was charged with bribery because he was part of the FBI sting known as Abscam. FBI agents dressed as Arab sheiks to set up a sting and catch members of Congress break the law with bribery charges. Williams was convicted and before he served twenty-one months in prison. He posted his resignation only because there were rumors of a possible expulsion proposal from the national Senate. But for Burton Wheeler, MT; Edward Gurney, FL; David Durenbeger, MN; and Ted Stevens, AK; even though they were either acquitted or had multiple forms of evidence of their corruption, never had any intention of resigning from their senate seat. Ted Stevens lost his senate in re-election but died in a plane crash in 2010.

But way after he was defeated in his re-election campaign, he stood as a national Senator all the way till the last day in office.

And, of course, the senator that still is remaining a national senator even though he is awaiting trial on bribery, conspiracy, and mail fraud. This is none other than Senator Bob Menendez of New Jersey. For a senator to remain representing New Jersey with that indicted rap sheet truly gives a bad name to the Garden State.

But the national Senate has willfully and hypocritically made rules against the will of the people and the sovereign State. This is the reason they have allowed a suspected criminal like Bob Menendez to remain in the Halls of Senate. We do know that in pre-1913, a national senator had a corrupt allegation, the state legislature of that State would recommend his resignation or dismissal. It was never in the minds of the framers to let Congress interfere in a matter of the State.

The corruption stories do not end with this New York Times article. The alleged corruption, post-Seventeenth Amendment has made and continue to make more headlines.

In 1989, financier and head of a savings and loans, Charles Keating, had connections in corrupt allegations towards five national senators, known as the Keating Five. Senators Dennis DeConcini, AZ; Alan Cranston, CA; John Glenn, OH; John McCain, AZ; and Don Riegle, MI. Charles Keating suffered more than the five senators that took funds from Keating's corporations. None of five senators were punished and one continue his life as a national senator, even unsuccessfully tried to run for president in 2008.

"Commit a crime, get no repercussions, and run for president" should have been McCain's presidential slogan.

It is the Seventeenth Amendment that creates a haven of criminals. These senators get away with any corrupt allegation because they now have created a populist ideology that they are untouchable because of their voting base. They hide their thievery by throwing funds at their base, and they continue to steal from the loot.

Nothing will ever change now, until the citizens see what the Seventeenth Amendment has done to our republic. It has brought dismay, confusion, chaos, and corruption to everyday use in America and Washington. If you think the Newberry case or the Vare case brought confusion into the hearts of each citizen, this case will get you very upsetting.

This case upsets me in the sense because they once again ignore the main pointer of the Seventeenth Amendment to pursue special interests for themselves and the federal government.

* * *

That the legislature of any State "**MAY**" empower the executive thereof to make temporary appointments until the people fill the vacancies by election as the legislature may direct. This Amendment shall not be so construed as to affect the election chosen before it becomes valid as part of the Constitution."

Has anybody read the text to the Seventeenth Amendment very carefully? This is what happens to our republic. Progressive radicals, regardless of party, act too hastily in changing our American political life that they do not encounter errors in the English language. This happens every time, they ram unconstitutional and unprincipled legislation with no regards to English composition into our beloved laws.

If the amendment has this sort of language to propose that the state legislatures of the several States "may" empower the executive to make temporary appointments. Then again, they "may not" empower the executive to make such appointments. Therefore, the state legislature "may" empower themselves to make such appointments when a vacancy occurs.

If the language suggests this power to be returned to the state legislatures, then we would not have that charade in 1991 Pennsylvania or 2008 Illinois.

The charade must continue to appease to the populist masses and create unnecessary drama across the nation where it is not needed, nor wanted.

"John Heinz, a United States Senator from Pennsylvania, died on April 4, 1991 in an airplane accident. A Pennsylvania statute, 25 Pa.Stat.Ann. Section 2776 (Purdon 1991), sets forth the procedure which should be applied to fill a senatorial vacancy. That statute provides, inter alia, that the Senator's unexpired term is to be filled by a special election to be held at the time of the next general or municipal election occurring at 90 days after the happening of the vacancy. The Governor is obliged to issue writs of election within 10 days after the vacancy happens." (Opinion of the Court of Trinsey v. Pennsylvania; United States Court of Appeals. Third District, by Chief Judge Sloviter, 1991).

"In accordance with that statute, the Governor of Pennsylvania, Robert P. Casey, issued a writ of election declaring a special election for November 5, 1991; on May 13, 1991, Governor Casey named Harris Wofford as a temporary appointment to fill the senatorial vacancy." (Opinion of the Court of Trinsey v. Pennsylvania; United States Court of Appeals. Third District, by Chief Judge Sloviter, 1991).

The statute of the Keystone state is quite clear per the instructions to follow from the Seventeenth Amendment. Except from one detail that is completely erroneous. The governor of the State is not "obliged" to appoint a temporary appointment. The governor, with the instruction of the state legislature picks the temporary senate appointment. In reading that language of the amendment, I am beginning to doubt that the power given by the legislature can be stripped and returned to the State.

"The statutory provision of principal relevance to the issues in this appeal provides: "Candidates to fill vacancies in the office of the United States Senator shall be nominated by political parties, in accordance with party rules relating to the filling of vacancies, by means of nomination certificates" to be filed at least 60 days prior to the special election." (Opinion of the Court of Trinsey v. Pennsylvania; United States Court of Appeals. Third District, by Chief Judge Sloviter, 1991).

"The Democratic and Republican parties are the only parties which fit this definition at least at this time. Individuals or candidates of other political parties must satisfy the state's requirements as to nomination papers in order to appear on the ballot for the special election. *Id.*, Section 2911(a)-(d). Section 2776 provides that the Governor may make a temporary appointment to fill the vacancy until the special election." (Opinion of the Court of Trinsey v. Pennsylvania; United States Court of Appeals. Third District, by Chief Judge Sloviter, 1991).

In reading the full PA., Stat., Ann., Section 2776 regarding filling vacancies for open senate seats, does seem to show privilege under law for major political parties and denying equal protection of the law to individuals and third political parties. The Seventeenth Amendment has set a bad precedent towards the republic in equal participation in the political process.

"On April 29, 1991, John S. Trinsey, Jr., filed a complaint in the United States District Court for the Eastern District of Pennsylvania, alleging that he wishes to become a candidate to fill the vacancy caused by Senator Heinz's death, and asserting that section 2776 violates the Fourteenth and the Seventeenth Amendments of the Constitution because it authorizes nominations of candidates to fill senate vacancies by political parties rather than by primary elections." (Opinion of the Court of Trinsey v. Pennsylvania; United States Court of Appeals. Third District, by Chief Judge Sloviter, 1991).

"The district court's analysis began with the undisputable proposition that the constitutional right of the citizens of Pennsylvania to vote for their national representatives has its foundation in the Qualifications Clauses in Article I of the Constitution, U.S. Cons., art., I, Section 2, clause 2, and the Seventeenth Amendment. The Qualifications Clause of Article I applies only to the election of members of the House of Representatives and thus is inapplicable here. Instead, we are concerned with the Seventeenth Amendment, which contains provision for election of United States Senators by state legislatures with a provision requiring popular election of Senators. The district court analyzed the legislative history of the Seventeenth Amendment and numerous federal cases under the First, Fourteenth, and Fifteenth Amendments. The district court stated that "the [Supreme] Court has recognized that the Constitution guarantees the franchise at all stages of the electoral process, including thew nomination stage." Typescript Op. 9. The court noted that the right to vote is fundamental and is protected against private as well as state interference. The court recognized, however, that the issue whether the right to vote must be protected at the nomination stage has not been squarely presented before. Indeed, it concluded from the Supreme Court precedence that "[i]t is clear that the states could choose to run general elections [without] the prior selection of major political party nominees by primary or otherwise." (Opinion of the Court of Trinsey v. Pennsylvania; United States Court of Appeals. Third District, by Chief Judge Sloviter, 1991).

The right to vote has never been discouraged whether in a primary election setting or general election setting. The question is not if the right to vote has been denied to Mr. John S. Trinsey.

The question is whether if the Seventeenth Amendment gives Congress the power to regulate a state's power in elections, whether primary, general and/or special.

"The district court relied primarily on the Seventeenth Amendment. The language itself, as the district court acknowledged, contains no reference to a primary election. The Seventeenth Amendment to the Constitution provides in relevant part:

When vacancies happen in the representation of any State in the Senate, the executive authority of such State shall issue writs of election to full such vacancies: Provided, That the legislature of any State may empower the executive thereof to make temporary appointments until the people fill the vacancies by election as the legislature may direct.

"Notwithstanding the lack of language referring to a primary, the district court discerned from the legislative history of the Seventeenth Amendment a congressional intent to treat "nomination as a part of the general electoral process," Typescript Op. at 8, and it was therefore "reluctant to hold that the framers of the Seventeenth Amendment were authorizing major political parties to choose their nominees without an election." *Id.*, at 9. We do not believe the legislative history supports the construction placed upon it by the district court."

(Opinion of the Court of Trinsey v. Pennsylvania; United States Court of Appeals. Third District, by Chief Judge Sloviter, 1991).

There is also a lack of language referring to a general, or special. One thing that the amendment gives the right to the State to set control the rules of the electoral process. Here the amendment's language that is troubling me is that they may allow the governor of the State to make an appointment. The troubling word is *may*. I believe that the state legislature still has that right to may or may not allow that power to the executive.

"The district court's holding that the Seventeenth Amendment requires the popular election of party nominees rested not only on excerpts from the legislative history but also on its reading of two Supreme Court cases, *United*

States v. Classic, 313 U.S. 299, 61 S. Ct. 1031, 85 L.Ed. 1368 (1941), and *Tashjian v. Republican Party of Connecticut*, 479 U.S. 208, 197 S. Ct. 544, 93 L.Ed. 2d. 514 (1986). The district court's opinion suggests that *Classic* and *Tashjian* establish the proposition that the right to nominate candidates through primaries, like the right to vote in a general election, is a right secured by the Constitution. We read those cases differently.

"Nothing in *Classic* suggests that the Constitution requires the holding of primaries in the election of representatives. Instead, the Court emphasized that the Constitution gave the States "wide discretion in the formulation of a system" for electing representatives. *Id*. At 311, 61 S.Ct. at 1035." (Opinion of the Court of Trinsey v. Pennsylvania; United States Court of Appeals. Third District, by Chief Judge Sloviter, 1991).

We reach a similar conclusion about *Tashjian v. Republican Party of Connecticut*, 479 U.S. 208, 197 S. Ct. 544, 93 L.Ed. 2d. 514 (1986), upon which this district court relied heavily. The Republican Party in Connecticut, which had adopted a rule which permitted independent voters to vote in Republican Party primaries for statewide and federal offices, challenged a Connecticut election law that required voters in primaries to be registered members of that party." (Opinion of the Court of Trinsey v. Pennsylvania; United States Court of Appeals. Third District, by Chief Judge Sloviter, 1991).

"A more fundamental problem with the district court's reliance on Tashjian and Classic is that those cases involved regular general elections, whereas section 2776 is concerned only with the special election of a successor to a vacancy in a Senate Seat." (Opinion of the Court of Trinsey v. Pennsylvania; United States Court of Appeals. Third District, by Chief Judge Sloviter, 1991).

The district court is mentioning in their opinion, the popular activity of an election rather than what the Amendment is currently constituting for governance. The two cases that the district court refers to is not the same to what the Pennsylvania statue section 2776 dictates. They are describing cases in where the voter was disfranchised in a primary election.

The Seventeenth Amendment shows no language of voter disfranchisement. Section of that amendment clearly states that when there is a vacancy of a senate seat, there must be appointment by the governor with the authority of the state legislature. Then the legislature must direct to a special election within a window after the seat has been vacant and filled by the governor's appointment.

I understand Mr. John S. Trinsey's frustration that he wants to run for a senate seat in his home state of Pennsylvania. But he would have been wise to read the amendment that he is suing before wasting the taxpayers' money of Pennsylvania and for the nation.

"This vacancy proviso of the Amendment has been found to confer "a reasonable discretion upon the states concerning the timing and manner of conducting vacancy elections." *Valenti v. Rockefeller*, 292 F. Supp. 851, 866 (S.D.N.Y. 1968), aff'd, 393 U.S. 404, 405, 406, 89 S.Ct. 689, 693, 21 L.Ed.2d 635, 636 (1969). In *Valenti*, New York voters challenged the provision of the state election law that Senate vacancies which arise less than 60 days before the regular spring primary be filled at the general election in the next even-numbered year. As a result of the timing of Senator Robert F. Kennedy's death, the interim appointed selected by the Governor of New York to fill the Senate vacancy would serve some 29 months. The Plaintiffs argued that the Seventeenth Amendment gave authority for the Governor to make a temporary appointment as successor only until the vacancy can be filled by the people at the next regularly scheduled election, two years earlier under state law. The three-judge court in Valenti, summarily affirmed by the Supreme Court, rejected plaintiffs' argument that the Seventeenth Amendment compelled New York to adopt plaintiffs' proffered timetable for filling a Senate seat vacancy. Instead, the court held that the "natural reading" of the vacancy provision of the Seventeenth Amendment "grants to the States some reasonable degree of discretion concerning both the timing of vacancy elections and the procedures to be used in selecting candidates for such elections." (Opinion of the Court of Trinsey v. Pennsylvania; United States Court of Appeals. Third District, by Chief Judge Sloviter, 1991).

The Third Circuit is correct in reversing the decision and we will get to that conclusion in a moment. The Seventeenth Amendment should stand as it is written. Regardless that there is a differential political party in power in that State, the Constitution stands above first any political party or partisanship.

The death of Senator Heinz and the issue with this senate seat is the same precedent to what happened with the death of Senator R. F. Kennedy. The vacancy clause of the Seventeenth Amendment is not there to play partisan politics especially after the seat becomes available after the death of the current Senator. That is what this amendment will do to our republic. It will create deep partisanship ties and go against the basic and structured principles of our ailing American republic of sovereign States. That is what happened after the death of Senator Robert Kennedy and his seat became available. The state law of New York and with accordance with the Seventeenth Amendment is crystal and not unconstitutional. The governor at that time, Nelson Rockefeller, a Republican. He received instructions from the state legislature to appoint somebody to fill the vacant seat. Also, the state legislature gave instructions in commencing the special election right after the seat became open and filled.

The three-judge panel reviewing the case in New York and affirmed by the Supreme Court rejected the plaintiffs' case and sided with the Constitution. There is nothing more in this world to give me great pleasure for the Courts to disavow and discredit this unprincipled amendment. But I am a constitutionalist at best, and

I will rather see this amendment repealed in the Halls of Congress than in the Supreme Court's chambers.

In recent years, a distinct issue arose in 2009. The youngest brother of Senator Robert F. Kennedy and President John F. Kennedy, Senator Edward Kennedy was battling a terrible disease that was affecting his life, livelihood, and political career. In the final months, before he died on August 25, 2009, an ailing Senator Kennedy pleaded with Massachusetts state leaders to change a state senatorial vacancy law. This change that Senator Kennedy was adamantly lobbying the state legislators was to speed up the senate replacement if he would have to step down or died while serving this seat. The state law was passed and signed by then-Governor Mitt Romney, a Republican, and now the then-Governor Deval Patrick, a democrat, would benefit to have this law change to keep the senate appointment and possibly win the special election if they would have moved it to an earlier date. The state legislature of Massachusetts never changed the law, the governor appointed Paul G. Kirk to finish off the term left by Ted Kennedy. The special election took place on January 19, 2010, 147 days after the vacancy opened. The state law is the state law and with accordance to the Seventeenth Amendment.

In conclusion, politicians cannot submit to partisanship to overcome their special interests. But that is what the Seventeenth Amendment brings out to everybody. A thirst for personal greed and disenfranchisement towards federalism. The language is clear and must be respected. All the amendments at present time, must be read, understood, and followed without any hints of partisanship or special interests.

"In sum, we have found nothing in the legislative history of the Seventeenth Amendment or in the Supreme Court cases relied upon by the district court that supports a conclusion that a state is constitutionally bound to hold a primary for nominations to fill a senatorial vacancy, either because it has a procedure for primaries in general elections or because it has given political parties some role in the nomination process." (Opinion of the Court of Trinsey v. Pennsylvania; United States Court of Appeals. Third District, by Chief Judge Sloviter, 1991).

"Not only does the proviso state that the state legislature "may" empower the executive to make temporary appointments but, in language which itself could be deemed dispositive of the issue before us, it also states that those interim appointments will continue until filled by an election "as the legislature may direct." U.S. Const. amend. XVII." (Opinion of the Court of Trinsey v. Pennsylvania; United States Court of Appeals. Third District, by Chief Judge Sloviter, 1991).

"Once we conclude that the Seventeenth Amendment does not mandate that Pennsylvania conduct a primary before holding a general election to fill a senatorial vacancy, it follows that there is no fundamental right infringed by the Pennsylvania statute at issue." (Opinion of the Court of Trinsey v. Pennsylvania; United States Court of Appeals. Third District, by Chief Judge Sloviter, 1991).

As I quite stated, the language of the amendment and the Pennsylvania statute supporting the amendment, stands firm against the plaintiff, John S. Trinsey. Appointments by the governor, instructed by the state legislature, and organizing the special election is what the amendment states. The amendment has no mention of primary or general elections.

I brought this type of language in my beginning discussion of this case, and I point it out again, because it is very valuable to know and learn what words mean. The amendment states that "the state legislature "may" empower the executive to make necessary appointments." Let's truly examine the word "may". In Merriam Webster's dictionary definition term of this word, states "have permission to". And yet again, you can add the adverb "not" to deny the "have permission to". In the end, the state legislature "may" or "may not" give permission to the executive to make temporary appointments. I believe there is a huge window of correctness and someone needs to file a challenge on this misrepresentation of simple English vocabulary. Because of this, I believe the sovereign state legislatures "may" return to give permission to themselves to make necessary appointments to an open senate seat and not the executive. They also remain to have the power to schedule to call a special election at their discretion.

I have a major issue in how the amendment has written this clause that "the state legislature "may" empower the executive to make the appointments" at the executive's discretion and advise of his appointment.

The Constitution cannot predict crooks, but the Seventeenth Amendment has indeed introduced them to the Constitution. I am talking about the latest major scandal; this amendment has produced. The 2008 electoral victory of Senator Barack H. Obama to the presidency. Therefore, his seat had to be vacated and then the state legislature with their power allowed the executive to appoint a senator. Enter Governor of Illinois Rod Blagojevich. When President-elect Obama handed in his resignation to his senate seat, the vacant seat became Blagojevich's own special interest bidding war for that seat.

"I've got this thing and it's f***ing golden, and uh, uh, I'm just not giving it up for f***in' nothing. I'm not gonna do it. And, and I can always use it. I can parachute me there."

– Former Governor Rod Blagojevich caught in a wiretapped phone call.

"Unless I get something real good [in exchange], s**t, I'll just send myself, you know what I'm saying," Blagojevich said one day before Obama's election, unaware that he was being wiretapped. (Illinois governor charged with taking bribes for Obama's Senate seat, Elana Schor in Washington, The Guardian, December 9, 2008.).

The authors of the Seventeenth Amendment never once pondered that their amendment would explode with full corruption and defrauding from a state public official. Yet again, this is what we the state, respectively the people cannot give authority to one public official while restricting it to the state legislature. With a balance of authority among the legislature, they are indeed checked more than one individual.

The executive has been given a power to choose wisely for the better and benefit of their state, not to prey on how to finance their special interests on behalf of the national Senate, the States true representative assembly in Washington.

The power of state sovereignty has not been entirely lost. The people and respectively the State need to read quite well the amendment's language. This could be a moment in truly returning its full sovereign rights back to the States.

Federal and State of Illinois authorities had evidence against Governor Blagojevich in trying to bribe for a national senate seat and brought him up on corruption charges.

The state legislature, on December 15, 2008, voted in favor of impeachment proceedings against their governor. Rod Blagojevich was impeached by the Illinois State House of Representatives and later convicted by the State Senate and removed from office.

After the sun laid in dark times in the Prairie State. Honesty and truth decided to light up that state. But nothing has changed in the "Land of Lincoln," because Illinois has covered their corrupt tracks and continues to be even more corrupt to this day, just smarter crooks to find loopholes within the Seventeenth Amendment.

When I read about this latest corruption case involving an executive official taking bribes for a senate replacement appointment. I asked myself, if truly a state legislature would have done this as one man tried to do and tried to get away with it. I doubt it because it is hard to hide from one group than one individual. Blagojevich tried to hide it and to this day, still believes he is innocent of these crimes. This is one excellent reason to try to repeal this vile, unprincipled amendment to be rid of the sole corrupt element that chooses for the state's representation. This is also one more reason to carefully read the language of the amendment and ask yourself, "Does the legislature have to give this power to the governor?" I say no and let the state legislatures reclaim this power.

I am going to bring up John S. Trinsey's claim that this special election violated his equal protection rights under the Fourteenth Amendment.

"Relying upon that primary votes must be weighed equally, the court stated that "[b]ecause the statute allows parties to make distinctions that deny him his right to vote, Trinsey has an equal protection claim as a voter." (Opinion of the Court of Trinsey v. Pennsylvania; United States Court of Appeals. Third District, by Chief Judge Sloviter, 1991).

"...we cannot find any Equal Protection violation in Pennsylvania's decision to leave the nomination procedure to Party rules that in effect disenfranchise the Party's members." (Opinion of the Court of Trinsey v. Pennsylvania; United States Court of Appeals. Third District, by Chief Judge Sloviter, 1991).

No one is denying John S. Trinsey's equal protection right as a voter. He does not have equal protection claim as a candidate. The Seventeenth Amendment makes that clear in the Vacancy clause and special election clause.

He can run in the special election, but the state legislature made the rules clear for party nominees, for special elections for a vacant seat, not to be confused with primary or general elections.

The United States of America truly began as a Roman Republic dream that later became a Roman Empire nightmare. The senators were once servants of the state, but later they turned out to become owners of the people of their respective state. The senators became beholden not to the state but to conglomerate business monopolies and to their own special interest greed. Each senator disregarded the issues of their state and became a representative and beholden to other forms of representation. The progressives of that time, same as the progressives of today, ruined and are ruining this "a more perfect union republic" by increasing the size of the central government. That in the end, they have made the citizens pay dearly for it with their forced contribution by way of collected income tax.

You and I can only hope that we return to the sanity of the old American republic principled way of life. But the damage has deepened the wound and we may never heal the wound properly again. It was one dream that our Founding Fathers had for the newly made nation, and in a split second it was shattered by greedy, ambitious, and inconsiderate progressives who did not live up to the standards of our Founding Fathers. Again, one could only hope that we heal this damage and regain back our American "Roman" Republic.

There have been a few people that have made the claim to repeal this amendment from our Constitution. For those who speak for liberty are shut out and discarded because of speaking the truth.

One person that spoke about a possible repeal of the Seventeenth Amendment is a very own former national senator. Senator Ben Sasse of Nebraska.

"In a Wall Street op-ed titled "Make the Senate Great Again," Sasse called for an end to the amendment, among other changes to the Senate "aimed at promoting debate, not ending it." He also recommended abolishing standing committees, requiring senators to show up for floor debates, implementing 12-year term limits, and requiring senators to live together in dorms when in Washington. "What would the Founding Fathers think of America if they came back to life?" Sasse wrote. "Their eyes would surely bug out first at our technology and wealth. But I suspect they'd also be stunned by the deformed structure of our government. The Congress they envisioned is all but dead. The Senate in particular is supposed to be the place where Americans hammer out our biggest challenges with debate. That hasn't happened in decades—and the rot is bipartisan." Before the 17th Amendment was ratified in 1913, Article I of the Constitution mandated that each state legislature vote to send two senators to Washington. Sasse argues that returning control to state legislatures would be a way of increasing local control in the Senate in a time of polarization and nationalization in politics. "Different states bring different solutions to the table, and that ought to be reflected in the Senate's national debate," he wrote. "The old saying used to be that all politics is local, is but today—thanks to the internet, 24/7 cable news and a cottage industry dedicated to political addiction—politics is polarized and national. That would change if state legislatures had direct control over who serves in the Senate." The Nebraskan Senator also suggested ridding the Senate cameras because in the presence of cameras, Senators "aren't trying to learn from witnesses, uncover details, or improve legislation. They're competing for sound bites." "Without posturing for cameras, Republicans and Democrats cooperate on some of America's most complicated and urgent problems," he wrote."

(Ben Sasse Calls for Repealing the 17th Amendment, Eliminating Popular-Vote Senate Elections; Brittany Bernstein, September 9, 2020).

Senator Ben Sasse states some great points to repeal this unprincipled amendment and some points that I can do without if Congress or a state legislature brings forth a resolution for a repeal amendment.

Sasse proposes to repeal the amendment and installing some federal regulations onto the sovereign States. They are very similar regulatory legislations that were imposed, just after the civil war, like the Act of 1866. To require for national senators be present a quorum on the floor. This is exactly what the progressives of the middle of the Nineteenth century concocted with the Act of 1866. If the state legislature of Michigan cannot get their act together in sending their senatorial delegation to Washington City. Why should the session not proceed and damage the chances for other States to have a presence? Also, to require for national senators be forced to live together in dorms, this is not college, it is the national Senate. They should not be forced to live together by federal legislation, it should be given as a choice, not a restriction. Abolishing the standing committees, that is an act of the national senate itself, not an act for the sovereign State. I see no harm if the national Senate wishes to stream-line their committees.

Yes, all states are different, but they are all the same with one common cause in mind, the Constitution. They are built to be an American republic of sovereign States, not united for a common democracy cause. They should be united by the principles of the Constitution, not by federal highways, airports, railways, and canals.

After the Seventeenth Amendment was ratified, frankly every single Senator has received a celebrity status that they were never intended to have or achieved to become a national celebrity. Sasse is correct in this that today's senators are competing to achieve for charisma status rather than a political stature status. The media has changed and now the media grabs this unprincipled celebrity status to lift them up for them to become rogue and arrogant Caesarian tyrants. Hence why, I brought up the 1948 Texas Senate primary election.

Senator Ben Sasse is on the right track in breaking the mold to pursue an advancement for a repeal of this amendment. This amendment stole the state's sovereignty, and it must be returned. We do not want shady characters like Lyndon B. Johnson, Ralph O. Brewster, and Rod Blagojevich, taking the power away from the States and tucking it in their pockets filled with their own interests rather than the sovereign States.

But I feel the fight is far from over for the American people and I believe that we can regain their state powers if they put their faith, money, and influence in repealing this mess of these unprincipled amendments that is dismantling our American republic of sovereign States.

I truly call everybody to be on the alert that this amendment has done more damage than the Sixteenth Amendment alone. This amendment must be the first one to be repealed so we can once again breath the air of liberty and sovereignty across our several States of this American republic.

III.

The United States, even before becoming a republic, was firmly against centralized taxation policies for its citizens. Taxing citizens' income was not a founding principle of America. While the British colonial government imposed corporate taxes, it did not tax the colonists directly until introducing the Tea Tax and the Stamp Act. Once they started taxing the citizens to cover the expenses of the East India Company and other corporations, the citizens drew the line and entered a bloody conflict to gain independence and form a citizen-led, tax-free republic. The founding principle of the American Revolutionary War was to have freedom from a centralized authority government and taxation "with" proper representation.

The proper taxation with representation is when the government establishes a taxation policy that would benefit the citizen as well as the corporation. But that has never happened. The national government has entered an age of pure taxation policies and spending. But spending is another case, we are discussing taxation.

We have an entered an age of excessive taxation policies that benefit no American citizen. The only entity that benefits is the actual politician and the corporation seeking relief. The federal government has no authority to tax your income through direct taxation – from the beginning of this republic to this day.

The politicians in power and the political candidates seeking power in today's republic have been an abomination. They have been self-absorbed try to please their ego and gain favor with citizens by stating support for a decrease in taxation. They should be trying to eliminate the taxation burden onto the citizens.

There would be no burden if taxation were not embedded into the Constitution.

That is the main premise of these chapters in discussing taxation. To dive into the issue of taxation. We must start at the beginning of the dilemma – the beginning of a taxation policy against the citizens that was argued by the high court and later indoctrinated into our principled document. Later to be a burden of sanctioned robberies since 1913 with no accountability or honesty from our politicians, corporations, and citizens themselves.

To be clear, taxation of citizens' income done at the federal level is unconstitutional with or without amending the Constitution.

The power of taxation is granted to the sovereign states. But because there was an amendment, which remains constitutional but unprincipled, the federal government has exercised that authority. We are here to discuss the issue of the unprincipled form of taxation and its true unconstitutionality despite an amendment and the solution in returning this power to the sovereign states.

* * *

"In distributing the power of taxation(,) the Constitution retained to the States the absolute power of direct taxation, but granted to the Federal government the power of the same taxation upon condition that, in its exercise such taxes should be apportioned among the several States according to numbers; and this was done, in order to protect to the States, who where surrendering to the Federal government so many sources of income, the power of taxation, which was their principal remaining resource." (Syllabus of Pollock v. Farmers' Loan and Trust Company, 1895).

"It is the duty of the court in this case simply to determine whether the income tax now before it does or does not belong to the class of direct taxes, and if it does, to decide the constitutional question which follows accordingly, unaffected by considerations not pertaining to the case in hand." (Syllabus of Pollock v. Farmers' Loan and Trust Company, 1895).

The court has a duty to question the validity of a congressional act. The justices must ensure laws align with the powers constitutionally granted to the federal government. Federal powers are specific and enumerated, whereas state powers are broad and undefined. The court recognizes this and should act accordingly. However, recently, the Supreme Court and the other two branches of the federal government have overlooked this, implementing policies that contradict both the Constitution and federalism principles. "Taxes on personal property, or on income or on the income of personal property, are likewise direct taxes." (Syllabus of Pollock v. Farmers' Loan and Trust Company, 1895).

"The tax imposed by sections twenty-seven and thirty-seven, inclusive, of the act of 1894, so far as it falls on the income of real estate and of personal property, being a direct tax within the meaning of the constitution, and, therefore, unconstitutional and void because not apportioned according to representation, all those sections, constituting one entire scheme of taxation, are necessarily invalid." (Syllabus of Pollock v. Farmers' Loan and Trust Company, 1895).

Before 1913, the Supreme Court often acted in favor of protecting the sovereign rights of a state, as seen when they struck down a case in 1895. However, post-1913, the court's stance shifted, upholding rulings that expanded federal government powers under the Sixteenth Amendment. Any amendments are the purview of Congress to propose, with states having the final say in ratification.

In 1895, when the aforementioned case was nullified, many viewed it as a triumph for federalism. It served as a strong rebuke to members of Congress who sought to overstep their constitutional bounds. Even though an amendment now allows direct taxation, making it constitutional, many still consider the concept fundamentally flawed.

"In *Briscoe v. Commonwealth Bank*, 8 Pet. 118, and *City of New York v. Miln*, 8 Pet. 120, 122, this rule was announced by Chief Justice Marshall in the following language: "The practice of this Court is, not (except in cases of absolute necessity) to deliver any judgment in cases where constitutional questions are involved, unless four judges concur in opinion, thus making the decision that of a majority of the whole court. In the present cases four judges concur in opinion as to the constitutional questions which have been argued. The court therefore direct these cases to be reargued at the next term, under the expectation that a larger number of judges may then be present." (Rehearing of Pollock v. Farmers' Loan and Trust Company, 1895).

Regarding these two cases, I must agree with Chief Justice Marshall, which happens rarely. The Court must discuss the question of constitutionality for all legislative acts – national and state.

In the Briscoe case, the law is deemed constitutionally valid. States cannot issue currency or credit without approval from the federal Treasury Department.

Similarly, the *Miln* case finds its law constitutionally sound. This ruling allows states the authority over commerce and the right to accept or deny entry of foreign nationals and citizens within their borders.

Before 1913, cases concerning taxation on personal property or income posed valid constitutional questions and typically required consensus from the majority of the court. Cases post-1913 also raised valid constitutional concerns, with many arguing that such tax policies are unprincipled. While this is a separate debate, the sentiment persists.

The United States is distinct from other nations. The federal government has specific powers, while individual states retain their own authorities, including the power of taxation. The Founders, wary of granting too much power to a central authority, especially after witnessing abuses in centralized taxation systems, never intended for the national congress to impose taxes on personal incomes. Instead, they delegated this responsibility to individual states, leaving each to exercise its discretion.

Virginia – In 1786, a tax was imposed upon attorneys, merchants, physicians, surgeons, and apothecaries. 12 Henning's Statutes, 283; 13, 114. In 1793, the tax on city property was "five-sixths of one per cent of the ascertained or estimated yearly rent or income." Act of 1793, Shepherd's Stat. at Large, Va., 1792, 1802, 1, 224; American State Papers, 1 Finance, 481.

Vermont – *Cattle and horses, money on hand or due,* and obligations to pay money. Assessments proportioned to the profits of all lawyers, traders, and owners of mills, according to the judgment of discretion of the listers or accessors (p. 418).

New Hampshire – Stock in trade, *money* on hand or *at interest* more than the owner pays interest for, and all *property in public funds*, estimated at its real value; mills; *wharves; ferries at one-twelfth part of their yearly net income, after deducting repairs.*

Massachusetts – Vessels, stock in trade, securities, *all moneys* on hand or *placed out at interest* exceeding the sum due on interest by the individual creditor; silver plate, *stock owned by stockholders in any bank,* horses, cattle and swine (p. 420).

Rhode Island – Polls and the collective mass of property, both real and personal (p. 422).

Connecticut – Stock, carriages, plate, clocks. And watches, *credits on interest* exceeding the debts due on interest by the individual creditors; assessments apportioned to the estimated gains or profits arising from any and all lucrative professions, trades, and occupations. (p. 423).

New York – Assessments in the towns determined by a discretionary estimate of the collective and individual wealth of corporations and individuals (p. 425).

Delaware – Taxes have been hitherto collected of the estimated annual income of the inhabitants of the State, with reference to specific objects. A statute has been passed during the past year declaring that all real and personal property shall be taxed; provision is made for ascertaining the stock of merchants, traders, mechanics, and manufacturers for the purpose of regulating assessments upon and *estimated at one hundred pounds for every eight pounds of rent. Rents of houses and lots of cities, towns and villages at one hundred pounds for every twelve pounds of rent reserved* (p. 429).

Maryland – Taxes are imposed on the mass of property in general, there are licenses for attorneys at law for admission to the bar, and the like sum annually during his continuance to practice; licenses to retail spirituous liquors; to keep taverns; for marriage (p. 430).

Virginia – a tax on lots and houses in towns, and the tenant or proprietor was required to disclose on oath or affirmation the amount of rent paid or received by them respectively; ordinary licenses; slaves; stud horses and jackasses, ordinary licenses, billiard tables, legal proceedings (pp. 431, 432).

Georgia – Stock-in-trade, funded debt of the United States, slaves, all professors of law or physic and all factors and brokers, billiard tables (p. 436).

(Rehearing of Pollock v. Farmers' Loan and Trust Company, 1895).

"It is not, however, a tax on rentals on rentals at all. It is not a tax measured by anything present. It is measured simply by the taxpayer's ability to pay as indicated by his income for the previous year. The rentals have become moneys inextricably mingled with the other funds of the taxpayer." (Rehearing of Pollock v. Farmers' Loan and Trust Company, 1895).

The progressive movement, irrespective of party or affiliation, tends to emphasize the evident while overlooking constitutional nuances. In our republic, made up of sovereign states, the distinctions are unmistakable.

Before the case in question (and notably before 1913), no constitutional directive granted the federal government explicit taxation powers. Instead, this authority rested with the individual states and, by extension, the people. Tax mandates from these states stand as a clear constitutional endorsement. Conversely, directives by the national congress cast doubts on their constitutionality.

There are two primary methods to overturn a congressional act deemed unconstitutional: one involves the court's ruling it so, and the other allows states to enact resolutions, refusing compliance and nullifying the questionable act.

Since the 1787 Constitution became the guiding document for our republic, there has been misinformation and misunderstanding. Both federal politicians and some state legislators appear to endorse expanding national government powers. However, this was never the intention from the republic's inception, from its initial to its subsequent governing document. While the language can be inclusive and perplexing, the foundational philosophy remains consistent.

"The Constitution declares that "the Congress shall have the power to lay and collect taxes, duties, imposts and excises, to pay the debts and provide for the common defense and general welfare of the United States; but all duties, imposts and excises shall be uniform throughout the United States." Art. I, Sec. 8." (Dissenting Opinion of Pollock v. Farmers' Loan and Trust Company by Associate Justice John Marshall Harlan, 1895).

While I hold Justice Harlan in high regard, I differ in opinion regarding his dissent on taxation. Before 1913, Article 1, Section 8 didn't explicitly authorize Congress to levy a direct "income" tax on citizens. When the federal government does impose taxes, duties, and imposts, they must be consistent across the nation. The congressional tax acts scrutinized by the Court targeted specific regions or aspects of the country, and were not uniformly applied throughout the U.S. Additionally, the language of the clause and section did not specify a direct tax on citizen incomes.

"No capitation, or other direct, tax shall be laid, unless in proportion to the census or enumeration herein directed to be taken." Art. 1, Sec. 9. (Dissenting Opinion of Pollock v. Farmers' Loan and Trust Company by Associate Justice John Marshall Harlan, 1895).

"No tax or duty shall be laid on articles exported from any State." Art. 1, Sec. 9. (Dissenting Opinion of Pollock v. Farmers' Loan and Trust Company by Associate Justice John Marshall Harlan, 1895).

Justice Harlan is describing the monstrosity that came after 1913 – the enactment of the Sixteenth Amendment, which does not grant any power to the federal government to lay down direct taxation on people's income.

"The Fourteenth Amendment provides that "representatives shall be apportioned among the several States according to their respective numbers, counting the whole number of persons in each State, excluding Indians not taxed." (Dissenting Opinion of Pollock v. Farmers' Loan and Trust Company by Associate Justice John Marshall Harlan, 1895).

If anyone were to fully understand the language and meaning of the Fourteenth Amendment, it would no doubt be Justice Harlan. This amendment's primary goal is to ensure equality and lawful treatment for all citizens—whether native-born or naturalized—irrespective of race or color. It does not address taxation. Instead, it guarantees equal representation for all races both in Congress and within their respective state governments. "What are "direct taxes" within the meaning of the Constitution? In the Convention of 1787, Rufus King asked what the precise meaning of direct taxation was, and no one answered. Madison

Papers, 5 Elliot's Debates, 451. The debates of that famous body do not show that any delegate attempted to give a clear, succinct definition of what, in his opinion, was a direct tax. Indeed, the report of these debates is very meagre and unsatisfactory. An illustration of this found in the case of Gouvernour Morris. It is stated that on the 12th of July, 1787, he moved to add to a clause empowering Congress to vary representation according to the principles of "wealth and numbers of inhabitants," a proviso "that taxation shall be in proportion to representation." (Dissenting Opinion of Pollock v. Farmers' Loan and Trust Company by Associate Justice John Marshall Harlan, 1895).

"But, on the 8th of August, 1787, the work of the Committee on Detail being before the convention, Mr. Morris is reported to have re-marked, "let it not be said that direct taxation is to be proportioned to representation." 5 Elliot's Debates, 393." (Dissenting Opinion of Pollock v. Farmers' Loan and Trust Company by Associate Justice John Marshall Harlan, 1895).

Central to the Constitution, if we set aside the 16th Amendment, is the definition of "direct taxes." While Congress does possess the authority to levy taxes on the nation, it traditionally uses indirect taxation rather than directly taking from a citizen's income.

Gouverneur Morris posed an intriguing question, but it seems to come with ulterior motives. Subtly, he seems to lay the groundwork for the federal government to gain this power. Yet, he likely recognized the uphill battle, as before 1913, the Constitution genuinely prohibited direct taxation on personal income.

"We know of no reason for holding otherwise than that the words "direct taxes," on the one hand, and "duties, imposts and excises," on the other, were used in the Constitution in their natural and obvious sense. Nor, in arriving at what those terms embrace, do we perceive any ground for enlarging them beyond, or narrowing them within, their natural and obvious impact at the time the Constitution was framed and ratified." (Opinion the Court of Pollock v. Farmers' Loan and Trust Company by Associate Justice Chief Justice Melville Fuller, 1895).

The constitution is clear in its language:

"And, passing from the text, we regard the conclusion reached as inevitable, when the circumstances which surrounded the convention and controlled its action and the views of those who framed and those who adopted the Constitution are considered." We do not care to retravel ground already traversed; but some observations may be added." (Opinion the Court of Pollock v. Farmers' Loan and Trust Company by Associate Justice Chief Justice Melville Fuller, 1895).

The Constitution was adopted with unequivocal language concerning taxation. The Chief Justice's concluding remarks are concerning, as they hint to the progressive movement that there might be room for further constitutional adjustments. While I concede that there's scope for additions to the Constitution, they should be rooted in humanitarian causes. The ratification of the Thirteenth, Fourteenth, and Fifteenth Amendments were justifiable inclusions. However, introducing amendments without foundational principles is misguided and should not be championed. "In the light of the struggle in the convention as to whether or not the new Nation should be empowered to levy taxes directly on the individual until after the States had failed to respond requisitions—a struggle which did not terminate until the amendment to that effect, proposed by Massachusetts and concurred in by South Carolina, New Hampshire, New York, and Rhode Island, had been rejected—it would seem beyond reasonable question that direct taxation, taking the place as it did of requisitions, was purposely restrained to apportionment according to representation, in order that the former system as to ratio might be retained, while the mode of collection was changed." (Opinion the Court of Pollock v. Farmers' Loan and Trust Company by Associate Justice Chief Justice Melville Fuller, 1895).

From the outset, many sovereign states resisted the idea of a national body imposing taxes on citizens. If direct taxation by the federal government was dismissed in 1787, the concept should be even more contentious today.

The aftermath of the conflict between 1861 and 1865 saw the rise of an assertive federal government characterized by overreach and presumption. This era ushered in increased national intervention, from setting regulations to enforcing immigration and introducing new tax laws—all of which can be argued as unconstitutional.

As Americans, we should continually seek inspiration for governance from our founding principles. The Constitution provides a clear roadmap: many powers rest with individual states, with only a few designated to the federal government.

"This is forcibly illustrated by a letter of Mr. Madison of January 29, 1789, recently published, written after the ratification of the Constitution, but before the organization of the government and the submission of the proposed amendment to Congress, which, while opposing the amendment as calculated to impair the power, only to be exercised in extraordinary emergencies," assigns adequate ground for its rejection as substantially, since, he says, "every State which chooses to collect its own quota may always prevent a Federal collection, by keeping a little beforehand in its finances, and making its payment at once into the Federal treasury." (Opinion the Court of Pollock v. Farmers' Loan and Trust Company by Associate Justice Chief Justice Melville Fuller, 1895).

"The reasons for the clauses of the Constitution in respect of direct taxation are not far to seek. The States, respectively, possessed plenary powers of taxation." (Opinion the Court of Pollock v. Farmers' Loan and Trust Company by Associate Justice Chief Justice Melville Fuller, 1895).

This statement made by the Chief Justice makes quite clear that he understands the rules of federalism that govern this republic. He follows the wise words of the father of the Constitution, James Madison.

"If, in the changes of wealth and population in particular States, apportionment produced inequality, it was an inequality stipulated for, just as the equal representation of the States, however small, in the Senate, was stipulated for.

The Constitution ordains that each State shall have two members of that body, and negatively that no State shall by amendment be deprived of its equal suffrage in the Senate without its consent. The Constitution ordains affirmatively that representatives and direct taxes shall be apportioned among the several States according to numbers, and negatively that no direct tax shall be laid unless in proportion to the enumeration." (Opinion the Court of Pollock v. Farmers' Loan and Trust Company by Associate Justice Chief Justice Melville Fuller, 1895).

"The founders anticipated that the expenditures of the States, their Counties, cities, and towns, would chiefly be met by direct taxation on accumulated property, while they expected that those of the Federal government would be for the most part met by indirect taxes." (Opinion the Court of Pollock v. Farmers' Loan and Trust Company by Associate Justice Chief Justice Melville Fuller, 1895).

Initially, the framers stipulated equal representation for each sovereign state in the Senate, the upper house of Congress, and proportional representation based on population in the House of Representatives, the lower house. For genuine representation, there must be equality. Each state merits equal standing, just as each citizen does. Consequently, a senator, at a national level, represents the state itself, not a group of constituents in the populist sense. This viewpoint highlights the concerns with the 17th Amendment, which some argue has misconstrued the idea of representation. (I will delve deeper into this issue in subsequent chapters of my book.)

With equal representation comes equal taxation. Chief Justice Fuller outlined how the tax system should operate: states handle direct taxation within their territories, while the federal government covers its expenses via indirect taxation, which does not directly burden the citizen/consumer. The federal government can institute a direct tax, but it must be proportioned accurately to be legitimate.

The Whiskey Tax, which sparked the Whiskey Rebellion, was a justified levy on citizens. Its revenue was allocated properly to offset debts from the American Revolutionary War. Proper fiscal allocation results in transparent government accountability.

In 1894, Congress erred with the Wilson-Gorman Tariff, failing to allocate the tax correctly. This oversight led to its examination by the Supreme Court to determine its constitutionality.

In conclusion, the prerogative of direct taxation rests more with individual states than with the federal government. In a true Republic of sovereign states, which we claim to be, this is the essence. States hold vast, undefined powers, while the national government operates within specific, defined bounds.

"If the question propounded by Rufus King had been answered in accordance with the interpretation now given, it is not at all certain that the Constitution, in its present form, would have been adopted by the convention, nor, if adopted, that would have been accepted by the requisite number of States." (Dissenting Opinion of Pollock v. Farmers' Loan and Trust Company by Associate Justice John Marshall Harlan, 1895).

"A question so difficult to be answered by able statesmen and lawyers directly concerned in the organization of the present government, can now, it seems, be easily answered, after a reexamination of documents, writings, and treatises on political economy, all of which, without any exception worth noting, have been several times directly brought to the attention of this court." (Dissenting Opinion of Pollock v. Farmers' Loan and Trust Company by Associate Justice John Marshall Harlan, 1895).

Determining the constitutionality of an issue should be straightforward. The challenge often lies not with the question, but with politicians. If these officials thoroughly and accurately interpreted the Constitution, there would be fewer prolonged debates in court. Moreover, those who overly praise or even dramatize a founding father through mediums like Broadway may not fully grasp the Constitution's essence and the principles of federalism. "Hamilton, referring to the distinction between direct and indirect taxes, said it was "a matter of regret that terms so uncertain and vague in so important a point are to be found in the Constitution," and that would be vain to seek *for any antecedent settled legal meaning to the respective terms."* 7 Hamilton's Works, (orig. ed.,) 845." (Dissenting Opinion of Pollock v. Farmers' Loan and Trust Company by Associate Justice John Marshall Harlan, 1895).

Many are wary of individuals who seek to expand the national government's reach, potentially violating both the Constitution and states' sovereignty.

The Constitution outlines that while the National Congress has the power to impose direct taxation, it must be proportioned correctly to ensure a balance of power. Figures like Alexander Hamilton, however, often seemed poised to manipulate this power, potentially breaching the Constitution's intent.

The 1895 case was not the first instance where Congress attempted to impose a direct tax without proper apportionment to the states. The judgment from that year emphasized that the framers intended for states to wield the power of direct taxation, largely because they manage the related expenditures. It is not justifiable for one state to shoulder the costs of another's expenses when those costs are dictated by the federal government. For example, Massachusetts should not be burdened with Maine's seafood industry expenses.

The Constitution presents a complex scenario for the national government: Congress can impose a direct tax on its citizens, but the tax must be proportioned among states appropriately. This principle has been misapplied in the past, leading to claims of unconstitutionality. As a result, it's perhaps more prudent to let states handle direct taxation, while the national government manages other matters.

Justice Harlan's argument for national direct tax apportionment does not convincingly align with federalism principles. Direct taxes by Congress should be proportioned according to state populations, but states are not equal in many regards. This underscores the importance of entrusting this issue to individual states.

"For example, suppose two States, equal in census, to pay $80,000 each, by a tax on carriages of eight dollars on every carriage; and in one State there are 100 carriages and in the other 1000. The owners of carriages in one State would pay ten times the tax of owners in the other. A., in one State would pay for his carriage eight dollars, but B., in the other State, would pay for his carriage eighty dollars." "I think an annual tax on carriages for the conveyance of persons may be considered as within the power granted to Congress to lay duties." (Dissenting Opinion of Pollock v. Farmers' Loan and Trust Company by Associate Justice John Marshall Harlan, 1895).

The principle of apportioning taxes by the census population, as decreed by Congress, is a nuanced one. Justice Harlan's observation underscores that, while states might have similar populations, they don't necessarily have uniform economic capacities.

Take the hypothetical example of Pennsylvania and Mississippi. If Pennsylvania is mandated to pay ten times more per carriage than Mississippi, this does not account for the economic disparities between the states. This kind of federal mandate would be disproportionally burdensome for one state over the other, even if their populations were similar.

Such intricacies highlight the wisdom of the framers' decision to let individual states tailor their taxation systems according to their unique circumstances. Then, based on this self-determined system, states would contribute to the Federal Treasury. As Madison articulated in his discussions on taxation, it's paramount to consider both population and the economic realities of each state when devising a fair taxation system.

"Mr. Madison and Mr. Ames are the only speakers on that day reported in the Annals. "Mr. Madison objected to this tax on carriages as an unconstitutional tax; and as an unconstitutional measure, he would vote against it." (Opinion the Court of Pollock v. Farmers' Loan and Trust Company by Associate Justice Chief Justice Melville Fuller, 1895).

"Where did Mr. Hamilton stand? At that time, he was Secretary of the Treasury, and it may therefore be assumed, without proof, that he favored the legislation. But upon what ground? He must, of course, have concluded that it was not a direct tax. Did he agree with Fisher Ames, his personal and political friend, that the tax was an excise? The evidence is overwhelming that he did." (Opinion the Court of Pollock v. Farmers' Loan and Trust Company by Associate Justice Chief Justice Melville Fuller, 1895).

The ideological clash between the Virginians (primarily Jefferson and Madison) and the Hamiltonians (led by Alexander Hamilton) indeed laid the foundation for the first political parties in the United States. This divide manifested in the formation of the Federalists, who supported Hamilton's vision, and the Democratic-Republicans, who rallied behind the views of Jefferson and Madison.

Hamilton, the first Secretary of the Treasury, had a vision of a strong centralized government with a robust financial system underpinned by a national bank. He believed in the need for the federal government to assume state debts from the Revolutionary War and sought ways for the federal government to boost manufacturing and commerce. He believed in a liberal interpretation of the Constitution, which means reading between the lines and finding powers that might not be explicitly listed.

Jefferson and Madison, on the other hand, held a strict interpretation of the Constitution. They felt that if something was not expressly permitted in the Constitution, then it was prohibited. They advocated for states' rights and were highly skeptical of a national bank, viewing it as an overreach of federal power.

This foundational debate was not merely about policies but about the very nature and direction of the young American republic. While the labels and specific issues have evolved over time, the fundamental tensions—between centralized vs. decentralized power, urban vs. rural interests, and commerce vs. agrarianism—have continued to shape American politics in various forms.

Comparing the Virginians vs. Hamiltonians divide to modern political divides, like Trumpism vs. Bidenism, highlights the long-standing nature of ideological conflicts in American politics. However, it is worth noting that while the foundational debates were about the structure and scope of government in a nascent country, contemporary debates often involve a wider range of social, cultural, and economic issues.

This deep dive into the complexities of taxation in American history and its implications for federalism is a tapestry of historical events, constitutional debates, and ideological differences that provide a nuanced understanding of the tensions between state and federal powers.

From the Carriage Tax to the Wilson-Gorman Tariff, we have highlighted the interpretative challenges the judiciary faced in determining the scope and nature of direct taxation. Indeed, the late 19th century marked a pivotal time in the evolution of American governance, as the nation grappled with its post-Civil War identity and the role of the federal government in the broader tapestry of the republic.

Their feud might come to that effect when Congress passed a carriage tax and it went all the way to the high court for debate, exactly how the 1894 tax went to the high court, except this case resulted in favoring and pleasing the general government of the United States.

The Carriage Tax was labeled not to be a direct tax and therefore needed to be apportioned. As I stated to Justice Harlan's opinion on this tax, it was unjustly unapportion, because even though, it was justly founded equally under a census, there is still inequality in the law. If one federal law is not labeled as a direct tax but another one is, then what is the true role of the federal government on taxation? In the end, the question still stands, let's just say the Sixteenth Amendment is not mentioned in the constitution. Where does the federal government stand on the power of taxation?

That is the key question I am trying to find the answer to in this quest for federalism. The national government has been indeed tasked with the issue of taxation but in the sense of indirect taxation by way of tariffs or corporate taxation. In the sense of direct taxation, it has been quite complicated and alarming to have several court cases been brought to the high court for debate and discussion.

As of now, we are discussion if the National Congress has the power of direct taxation, with apportionment or not. The decision of the Carriage Tax was decided it was a direct tax and brought to the populist illusion that it was being apportioned. But the Wilson-Gorman Tariff was decided it was not a direct tax and not apportioned among the sovereign states.

There brought a lot of disillusionment with the 1895 decision among several Americans. We will broach the question at a later section of the book.

But we are now discussing the case that reshaped the republic that later brought the destruction, not only the political system but our economic and social culture of our dear American Republic.

This 1895 case really brought confusion, anger, sadness but most importantly brought confusion. This confusion happens when the national government encroaches onto the powers of the sovereign States and demands that power. Post-1865, Reconstruction posed unprecedented challenges and the general government of the United States took command of almost every power belonging to the states. This era, combined with the broader industrialization of the country, intensified the debates on the role and reach of the federal government. Several states were no help at all to stop the overreach of an abusive of power, but also the federal government were not the wiser either.

The 1895 case of *Pollock v. Farmers' Loan & Trust Co.*, ruled that federal income taxes on interest, dividends, and rents were direct taxes and thus unconstitutional unless apportioned. The case indeed underscored the continuing tensions between state and federal authority, especially in the realm of taxation.

"The truth is, that the articles taxed in one State should be taxed in another; in this way the spirit of jealousy is appeased, and tranquility preserved; in this way the pressure on industry will be equal in the several States, and the relation between the different objects of taxation [are] duly preserved." (Dissenting Opinion of Pollock v. Farmers' Loan and Trust Company by Associate Justice John Marshall Harlan, 1895).

I disagree with Justice Harlan about the role of the national government in taxation. Taxation is not a tool for equality, it is a tool for oppression.

A foundational tenet of federalism is that states maintain their sovereignty and distinctiveness within the framework of a national government. Indeed, the United States, as a federation of states, was built on the principle that while the national government would have certain enumerated powers, the states would retain a broad swath of authority over their internal matters. In the pre-1913 days, you cannot compare the sovereign states of New York to Florida or Pennsylvania to Missouri. Again, this is the beauty of our republic, each state is sovereign from one another and sovereign from the national government in directive policies – especially in a directive policy such as taxation. All sovereign states are equal in the eyes of the Constitution.

"Apportionment is an operation on States, and involves valuations and assessments, which are arbitrary, and should not be resorted to but in case of necessity. Uniformity is an instant operation on individuals, without the intervention of assessments, or any regard to States, and is at once easy, certain, and efficacious. All taxes on expenses or consumption are indirect taxes." (Dissenting Opinion of Pollock v. Farmers' Loan and Trust Company by Associate Justice John Marshall Harlan, 1895).

Apportionment is an important tool; however, the national Congress cannot broadly apportion or fail to apportion taxation policies across the entire republic, dividing tax and funds into specific regions. The manner in which the federal government apportions taxation policy to states is crucial. Many argue that the federal Carriage Tax was a pivotal moment in interpreting the American Constitution. Though it was deemed a direct tax, there were concerns about the appropriateness for carriage owners, even with census equality. The 1894 tax lacked clear apportionment among the states and was thus ruled unconstitutional. By that time, the U.S. had expanded beyond the original thirteen states, making the concept of apportioned taxes more complex and raising questions about the feasibility of a direct tax amendment to the Constitution. Justice Harlan's statement on uniformity sounds a bit arbitrary and arrogant. In legislative discussions or congressional debates, thorough assessments and careful consideration are essential when addressing taxation issues. No, I do not believe that all taxes on expenses and consumption are indirect taxes. Sovereign states are not beholden to the federal government, only if they choose to be by presenting legislation of that sort. The federal government can present legislation of indirect taxation.

"If a direct tax, it could only be laid in proportion to the census, which has not as vet been taken." (Dissenting Opinion of Pollock v. Farmers' Loan and Trust Company by Associate Justice John Marshall Harlan, 1895).

Justice Harlan is referring to the Carriage Tax, which was indeed a direct tax. In the eyes of the Constitution, the law is not justified and should be considered unconstitutional. Neither the Carriage Tax nor the Wilson-Gorman Tariff Act are constitutional Acts of Congress.

Justice Harlan is not being truthful in his statement. The law passed in 1795, affirmed by the court to be constitutional, then years later another direct federal tax law passed by congress, overturned by the court.

This is not the function that the framers envisioned for the tax structure for this republic. While creating chaos and dismay onto the states.

The constitutional framers did not condone this sort of bickering on who controls the financial structure of this nation. Especially the tax policy legislation.

Incidentally, the tax policy to be fully decided in one centralized location.

If the federal government are to take the reins in the tax policy system of our republic, then let them craft the law as it is specified in their enumerated constitutional powers. Power corrupts.

The year 1895 was the beginning of personal and corrupt political indulgences at the expense of the American citizenry and the use of a national congressional power with no constitutional power.

"Referring to certain observations of Madison, King, and Ellsworth in the convention of 1787, he said: "All this doubtless shows uncertainty as to the true meaning of the term 'direct tax'" but it indicates, also, an understanding that direct taxes were such as may be levied by capitation, and on lands and appurtenances, or, perhaps, by valuation and assessment of personal property upon general lists. For these were the subjects from which the States at that time usually raised their principal supplies. This view received the sanction of this court two years before the enactment of the first law imposing direct taxes *eo nominee*." (Dissenting Opinion of Pollock v. Farmers' Loan and Trust Company by Associate Justice John Marshall Harlan, 1895).

James Madison, a framer of the Constitution and its main author in 1787, comprehended the workings of federalism in the republic. He believed that states should have the discretion to levy direct taxes, while the national Congress handles indirect taxation. "The more intelligent adversaries of the new Constitution admit the force of this reasoning; but they qualify their admission, by a distinction between what they call *internal* and *external* taxations. The former they would reserve to the state governments; the latter, which they explain into commercial imposts, or rather duties on imported articles, they declare themselves willing to concede to the Federal head." (Opinion the Court of Pollock v. Farmers' Loan and Trust Company by Associate Justice Chief Justice Melville Fuller, 1895).

Many framers of the Constitution understood the distinct functions of government levels. As they crafted the republic, they recognized how to delegate the power of taxation. Chief Justice Fuller's majority opinion seemed to draw inspiration from James Madison's writings. Throughout history, some individuals have disregarded the original intent of taxation in our republic, seeking power by any means, even if it challenges constitutional principles. While some espouse constitutional values, they still lean towards a more expansive national government. A notable example is Alexander Hamilton." "In the thirty-sixth number, while still adopting the division of his opponents, he says: "The taxes intended to be comprised under the general denomination of internal taxes, may be subdivided into those of the *direct* and those of *indirect* kind . . . *As to the latter, by which must be understood duties and excises on articles of consumption,* one is at a loss to conceive, what can be the nature of the difficulties apprehended." (Opinion the Court of Pollock v. Farmers' Loan and Trust Company by Associate Justice Chief Justice Melville Fuller, 1895).

"Thus we find Mr. Hamilton, while writing to induce the adoption of the Constitution, *first,* dividing the power of taxation into *external* and *internal*, putting into the former the power of imposing duties on imported articles and into the latter all remaining powers; and, *second,* dividing the latter into *direct* and *indirect,* putting into the latter, duties on articles of consumption." (Opinion the Court of Pollock v. Farmers' Loan and Trust Company by Associate Justice Chief Justice Melville Fuller, 1895).

"It seems to us to inevitably follow that in Mr. Hamilton's judgment at that time all internal taxes, except duties and excises on articles of consumption, fell into the category of direct taxes." (Opinion the Court of Pollock v. Farmers' Loan and Trust Company by Associate Justice Chief Justice Melville Fuller, 1895).

People have differing opinions of Alexander Hamilton. Many believe him to be a man of political integrity and decency, but nothing could be further from the truth. Hamilton, in my opinion, is the first politician that advocated to do nothing in the lead up to the American Revolutionary War. To make matters worse, he made speeches and writings advocating for the opposite of what he really believed once in power. Alexander Hamilton is no hero to the American republic, but was in fact, a political scoundrel.

He once advocated for separation of taxation policies while this nation was being constructed. Then when he obtained power as

Treasury Secretary, he switched sides and advocated for more control to be given to the national government's financial institutions. Hamilton obtained power with a total disregard for the Constitution.

Therefore, I have no respect for anybody who praises Alexander Hamilton or for Hamilton himself. A man who advocated for the freedoms fought for to make this nation a reality and then later changes his mind is, in my opinion, a hypocrite and a liar.

If a federal tax policy were to be fully apportioned across all fifty states, consider the ramifications if it were unevenly distributed instead. Such policies could lead to significant financial, social, and political upheavals. The federal government's design intended to avoid favoritism toward any state, regardless of the birthplace of the chief executive or other federal civil servants. Favoritism, especially involving the financial resources of different states, was not the intended purpose. "The Constitution prohibits any direct tax, unless in proportion in numbers as ascertained by the census; and, in the light of the circumstances to which we have referred, is it not an evasion of that prohibition to hold that a general unapportion tax, imposed upon all property owners as a body for or in respect of their property, is not direct, in the meaning of the Constitution, because to the income therefrom?" (Opinion the Court of Pollock v. Farmers' Loan and Trust Company by Associate Justice Chief Justice Melville Fuller, 1895).

"Whatever the speculative views of political economists or revenue reformers may be, can it be properly held that the Constitution, taken in its plain and obvious sense, and with due regard to the circumstances attending the formation of the government, authorizes a general unapportion tax on the products of the farm and the rents of real estate, although imposed merely because of ownership and with no possible means from payment, as belonging to a totally different class from that which includes the property from whence the income proceeds?" (Opinion the Court of Pollock v. Farmers' Loan and Trust Company by Associate Justice Chief Justice Melville Fuller, 1895).

The Constitution of 1787 outlines that the national government can only collect direct taxes when they're apportioned based on census population among the sovereign States. However, for those deeply familiar with constitutional and Supreme Court documents, the practical implementation can seem more complex than its written form suggests. In practice, the guidelines can be perceived as challenging, perplexing, and fraught with pitfalls. We e cannot assign powers to the national government that are truly not specified in the Constitution. Because there is always an ambitious and corrupt federal civil servant that will always bypass the Constitution for his or her own personal indulgences.

It was better to have the enumerated taxation directive policy into the Constitution that the federal government, clearly stated that it was just to establish taxation for indirect means, and no mention of allowing direct taxation of any means in our principled document. And the direct taxation policies should be handled at the sovereign state level. I fear some of our constitutional framers wanted to have our Constitution dictated in some sort of a strange, arrogant language to confuse the American citizenry, leading it to be constitutionally deciphered in the courts and not in the Congress.

Since the founding and the pre-founding of this American Republic, the language of the law was always clear. The powers delegated were specifically divided onto the federal and state governments. Any new power added to the Constitution would be in the form of an amendment.

"The Congress of the Confederation found the limitation of the sources of the contributions of the States to "land, and the buildings and improvements thereon," by the eighth article of July 9, 1778, so objectionable that the article was amended April 28, 1783, so that the taxation should be apportioned in proportion to the whole number of white and other free citizens and inhabitants, including those bound to servitude for a term of years and three-fifths of all other persons, except Indians not paying taxes; and Madison, Ellsworth, and Hamilton in their address, in sending the amendment to the States, said: "This rule, although not free

> Anyone who is unaware of the delegated federal powers to the Constitution is uninformed, as well as arrogant.

from objections, is liable to fewer than any other that could be devised." 1 Ell, Deb. 93, 95, 98."

(Opinion the Court of Pollock v. Farmers' Loan and Trust Company by Associate Justice Chief Justice Melville Fuller, 1895).

Reflecting on Chief Justice Fuller's remarks, it's evident that he had a clear understanding of the workings of a centralized government. Even amidst the American Revolutionary War, the Continental Congress implemented a direct tax, ensuring its fair distribution among the soon-to-be sovereign states. This raises the question: If the founding framers could establish such a system, why did subsequent generations face challenges in upholding the same principle?

"According to the census, the true valuation of real and personal property in the United States in 1890 was $65,037,091, -197, of which real estate with improvements thereon made up $39,544,544,333. Of course, from the latter must be deducted, in applying these sections, all unproductive property and all property whose net yield does not exceed four thousand dollars; but, even with such deductions, it is evident that the income from realty formed a vital part of the scheme for taxation embodied therein. If that be stricken out, and also the income from all invested personal property, bonds, stocks, investments of all kinds, it is obvious that by far the largest part of the anticipated revenue would be eliminated, and this would leave the burden of the tax to be borne by professions, trades, employments, or vocations; and in that way what was the intention of Congress.

We do not mean to say that an act laying by apportionment [,] a direct tax on all real estate and personal property, or the income thereof, might not also lay excise taxes on business, privileges, employments, and vocations. But this is not such an act; and the scheme must be considered. Being invalid as to the greater part, and falling, as the tax would, if any part were held valid, in a direction which could not have been contemplated except in connection with the taxation considered as an entirety, we are constrained to conclude that sections twenty-seven to thirty-seven, inclusive, of the act, which became a law without the signature of the president on August 28, 1894, are wholly inoperative and void." Anyone who is unaware of the delegated powers to the Constitution are uninformed, as well as arrogant.

"Our conclusions may, therefore, be summed up as follows:

First. We adhere to the opinion already announced, that, taxes on real estate being indisputably direct taxes, taxes on the rents or income of real estate are equally direct taxes.

Second. We are of opinion that taxes on personal property, or on the income of personal property, are likewise direct taxes.

Third. The tax imposed by sections twenty-seven to thirty-seven, inclusive, of the act of 1894, so far as it falls on the income of real estate and of personal property, being a direct tax within the meaning of the Constitution, and, therefore, unconstitutional and void because not apportioned according to representation, all those sections, constituting one entire scheme of taxation, are necessarily invalid." (Opinion the Court of Pollock v. Farmers' Loan and Trust Company by Associate Justice Chief Justice Melville Fuller, 1895).

"Such a result is one deeply deplored. It cannot be regarded otherwise than as a disaster to the country. The decree now passed dislocated — principally, for reasons of an economic nature—a sovereign power expressly granted to the general government and long recognized and fully established by which judicial decisions and legislative actions. It so interprets constitutional provisions, originally designed to protect the slave property against oppressive taxation, as to give privileges and immunities never contemplated by the founders of the government." (Dissenting Opinion of Pollock v. Farmers' Loan and Trust Company by Associate Justice John Marshall Harlan, 1895).

"But the serious aspect of the present decision is that by a new interpretation of the

Constitution, it so ties the hands of the legislative branch of the government, that without an amendment of that instrument, or unless this Court, at some future time, should return to the old theory of the Constitution, Congress cannot subject to taxation—however great the needs or pressing the necessities of the government—either the invested personal property of the country, bonds, stocks, and investments of all kinds, or the income arising from the renting of real estate, or from the yield of personal property, except by the grossly unequal and unjust rule of apportionment among the States. Thus, undue and disproportioned burdens are placed upon the many, while the few, safely entrenched behind the rule are permitted to evade their share of responsibility for the support of the government ordained for the protection of the rights of all." (Dissenting Opinion of Pollock v. Farmers' Loan and Trust Company by Associate Justice John Marshall Harlan, 1895).

"I cannot assent to an interpretation of the Constitution that impairs and cripples the just powers of the National Government in the essential matter of taxation, and at the same time discriminates against the greater part of the people of our country." (Dissenting Opinion of Pollock v. Farmers' Loan and Trust Company by Associate Justice John Marshall Harlan, 1895).

"The practical effect of the decision to-day is to give to certain kinds of property a position of favoritism and advantage inconsistent with the fundamental principles of our social organization, and to invest them with power and influence that may be perilous to that portion of the American people upon whom rests the larger part of the burdens of the government, and who ought not to be subjected to the dominion of aggregated wealth any more than the property of the country should be at the mercy of the lawless." (Dissenting Opinion of Pollock v. Farmers' Loan and Trust Company by Associate Justice John Marshall Harlan, 1895).

In reconciling the majority opinion of Chief Justice Fuller and the dissenting view of Associate Justice Harlan, I find myself leaning towards the majority's perspective. The majority clearly delineates the powers of the national government in the realm of taxation. It acknowledges the federal authority to impose taxes, whether indirectly or through apportioned direct taxation. The ruling rightly deemed the contested act unconstitutional as it lacked appropriate apportionment. While I personally disagreed with the Carriage Tax being considered constitutional, I respect the court's judgment and adhere to its decision. Justice Harlan's concluding remarks leave me perplexed. His predictions for the republic's future, as expressed in these statements, seem to lean heavily into speculative and controversial territory. First, there is no "old theory to the Constitution" designed for America. There has been one single theory to the Constitution regarding taxation and it has been explained by the majority opinion of the court. The national government's power of taxation is defined and direct. It has been defined that it can be a direct tax but correctly apportioned to the sovereign states. Also, they have the power of indirect taxation by way of tariffs.

Justice Harlan's stance seems to favor a pathway for the progressive movement to allow the national government to implement unapportion taxation against the sovereign states. Advocating for an amendment that gives the national government the power to tax citizens' earnings without apportionment or restraint can be viewed by some as overstepping constitutional boundaries. Arguably, pushing for an amendment for direct tax legislation might be seen as a greater challenge to the American Republic's principles than an amendment promoting equality among its citizens. As much as I respect Justice Harlan, he was blinded to what was constitutional and what was not constitutional. This overruling of a federal direct tax law does not cripple or impair the general government. Rather, this ruling keeps the national government in in check, preventing overreach legislation on taxation without what was mentioned by the father of our Constitution.

Justice Harlan is right, taxation does create hatred and discrimination among our citizens. National direct taxation does not bring equality, or fairness, it only indulges in hatred and discrimination among the American citizenry.

Nobody is denying the true nature of the central government's business on the issue of taxation. Congress can pass direct taxation policies, but it must and be clear to show apportionment standards to the sovereign states that bind this republic. The constitutional framers found themselves in a Catch-22.

They gave the permission of the general government to pass direct taxation policies, but it came with strict assurances of apportionment census allowances.

When a national legislator gets greedy with power, he forgets the rules of federalism and installs the rules of tyranny.

The opinions of the high court are not constitutional amendments or legislation, but they must be respected either way as if they were. I may not agree with many high court rulings, but the justices will always have my respect. Regarding this ruling discussed and decided in 1895, I strongly support it and respect it.

"Nor are we impressed with the contention that, because in the four instances in which the power of direct taxation has been exercised, Congress did not see fit, to levy a tax upon personality, this amounts to such a practical construction of the Constitution that the power did not exist, that we must regard ourselves bound by it. We should regret to be compelled to hold the powers of the general government thus restricted, and certainly cannot accede to the idea that the Constitution has become weakened by a particular court of inaction under it." (Opinion the Court of Pollock v. Farmers' Loan and Trust Company by Associate Justice Chief Justice Melville Fuller, 1895).

Individuals unfamiliar with the delegated powers of the Constitution may not fully understand its intricacies. The Constitution does grant Congress the authority to enact direct tax legislation, provided it adheres to the principle of apportionment among the sovereign states. As previously mentioned, it's a nuanced issue, and such apportionment must be equitable and accurately reflective of census proportions. In the early days of the Republic, taxes such as the Whiskey Tax were indeed apportioned correctly. However, there was debate over the Carriage Tax. While the Supreme Court deemed it correctly apportioned, James Madison expressed disagreement with this judgment. The reason Madison, Chief Justice Fuller, and I disagree with the Carriage Tax judgment is that even though it was apportioned to census qualifications, it remains unequal because of the Census population of carriage percentages per state.

Therefore, this ruling does not jibe with what the Constitution states about the powers delegated to the national government on taxation. In 1895, the federal tax law under scrutiny was clear in its intent not to be apportioned among the sovereign States. Consequently, it was deemed unconstitutional either by the courts or by the states through nullification.

* * *

At the chapter's outset, we delved into how the Supreme Court delineated the federal government's role concerning tax policy directives. The Constitution empowers the federal government to impose duties and imposts on the sovereign States as indirect taxes. Additionally, the federal government can formulate direct tax policies, but they must be apportioned based on the sovereign States' census. If a tax policy is not apportioned correctly, it would be categorized as an indirect tax. A significant takeaway from this examination is that the power of levying direct taxes primarily rests with the sovereign States, not with the federal government. This clear demarcation underscores the delineation of responsibilities and powers the Court established for the U.S. general government concerning taxation. Let us now define the role of the sovereign states in dictating the policy of taxation, as well as other powers that are clearly defined for the states to enforce. In the 1895 Court decision, Chief Justice Fuller emphasized that sovereign States hold the intrinsic authority to tax. Furthermore, if a federal tax law is enacted, it becomes the sovereign State's responsibility to determine whether to comply or not. The word "nullification" has become non-existent in the American political dictionary and everyday use in our glorious American Republic. Ever since the American education curriculum system abandoned their civics lessons. And by introducing a new unprincipled term known as "social studies" lessons, the very fabric of our American republic of sovereign states has been forever lost.

State legislators have occasionally turned to the idea of nullification, which is often misunderstood as a treasonous act against the national government. However, nullification is not synonymous with secession. Instead, it represents a state's constitutional right to decline cooperation with federal mandates they view as unconstitutional. This principle is rooted in the beliefs of several Constitutional Framers like Thomas Jefferson, James Madison, and Luther Martin. For instance, during the mid-1800s, nullification was used as an argument against the controversial Fugitive Slave Act. If this concept was introduced and thoroughly understood during one's educational journey, it might have played a significant role in preserving the ideals of the American Republic, championing both liberty and federalism. People are unaware that in 1798, two sovereign states sought to find liberty against a national government measure that targeted federal enforcement of the Naturalization Clause. The two sovereign states of Virginia and Kentucky sought fit to challenge the Alien and Sedition Act by refusing to cooperate with federal union officials. While the sovereign state of Massachusetts, the home of the second President, John Adams, sought to cooperate, which is the right of a sovereign state, it nonetheless truly defeats the purpose of the rules of federalism.

Then, in the mid-1800s, he slavery issue was becoming controversial, not only among the sovereign states but also across the world. Many sovereign states in the North began to pass nullification legislation against the federal legislation known as the Fugitive Slave Law. It is sad that the high court of the land headed by a rogue, arrogant, and racist Chief Justice Roger Taney shot down the very idea of the fabric of American federalism.

Following the Civil War, the federal government expanded its role, asserting greater authority under the guise of protecting citizens' civil rights. This shift was seen by many as the national government's attempt to enhance its scope in the name of national security. As this transition occurred, the sovereign States' drive to utilize nullification waned, leading them to cede more power to the federal government. This resulted in the federal government gaining authorities that were not originally enumerated to it.John C. Calhoun, while controversial for his unwavering support of a labor system that remains a dark chapter in American history, held firm beliefs in state sovereignty, nullification, and federalism. Often regarded as an "heir" to the Founding Fathers, his perspectives on these matters are of significance. In this discussion, the focus will be on Calhoun's advocacy for state nullification against federal taxation policies that impacted sovereign states. "A deep constitutional question lies at the bottom of this controversy. The question at is: Has this Government a right to impose burdens on the capital and industry of one portion of the country, try, not with a view to revenue, but to benefit another?" (Against the Force Bill, by John C. Calhoun, 15 & 16 February 1833).

John C. Calhoun raised questions about the role of the federal government in tax collection, highlighting potential dangers of a centralized government infringing on the rights of states and their citizens regarding income collection. Such a question, reflective of deep concerns about national tax policy, would have been pertinent during the 1895 Supreme Court oral argument of the Pollock Case of 1894. "The Federal Government has, by an express provision of the Constitution, the right to lay imposts. The State has never denied or resisted this right, nor even thought of so doing. The

Government has, however, not been contended with exercising this power as she had a right to do, but has a step beyond it, by laying imposts, not for revenue, but protection. This the State considers as an unconstitutional exercise of power—highly injurious and oppressive to her and the other staple States, and has, accordingly, met it with the most determined resistance. I do not intend to enter, at this time, into the argument as to the unconstitutionality of the protective system. It is not necessary. It is sufficient that the power is nowhere granted, and that, from the journals of the convention which formed the Constitution, it would seem that it was refused. In support of the of the journals, I might cite the statement of Luther Martin, which has already been referred to, to show that the convention, so far from conferring the power on the Federal Government, left to the State the right to impose duties om imports, with the express view of enabling the several States to protect their own manufacturers." (Against the Force Bill, by John C. Calhoun, 15 & 16 February 1833).

John C. Calhoun raised questions about the role of the federal government in tax collection, highlighting potential dangers of a centralized government infringing on the rights of states and their citizens regarding income collection. Such a question, reflective of deep concerns about national tax policy, would have been pertinent during the 1895 Supreme Court oral argument of the Pollock Case of 1894. The federal government was not primarily established to levy imposts and duties for the protection of the sovereign states. Each state traditionally maintained its own militia for defense. However, over time, the term "protection" evolved and is now often referred to as "National Security." To understand the distribution of power between the national and state governments, it is essential to examine the most recent amendment to our Bill of Rights.

"Those who make this objection overlook, I conceive, an important provision of the Constitution. By turning to the tenth amended article, it will be seen that the reservation of power to the States is not only against the powers delegated to Congress, but against the United States themselves, and extends, of course, as well to the judiciary as to the other departments of the government. The article provides that all powers not delegated to the United States, or prohibited by it to the States, are reserved to the States respectively, or to the people. This presents the inquiry: What powers are delegated to the United States?" (Against the Force Bill, by John C. Calhoun, 15 & 16 February 1833).

Calhoun outlined the specific powers designated to the federal government and the states. He emphasized the power of treaties in foreign relations, noting that just as the national congress can declare a treaty null and void, a sovereign state also possesses the authority to nullify an act of Congress if deemed unconstitutional. This chapter specifically delves into the delegated power of taxation. Calhoun's firsthand experiences with tax issues, both in Washington City and South Carolina, provide valuable insights into the matter. "Looking back, even at this distant period, with all our experience, I perceive but two errors in the act: the one in reference to iron, and the other minimum duty on coarse cottons. As to the former, I conceive that the bill, as reported, proposed a duty relatively too low, which was still further reduced in its passage through Congress. The duty, at first, was fixed at seventy-five cents the hundred-weight; but, in the last stage of its passage, it was reduced, by a sort of caprice, occasioned by an unfortunate motion, to forty-five cents. This injustice was severely felt in Pennsylvania, the State, above all others, most productive of iron, and was the principal cause of that great nation which has since thrown her so decidedly on the side of protective policy." (Against the Force Bill, by John C. Calhoun, 15 & 16 February 1833).

"The other error was that as to the coarse cottons, on which the duty was as much too high as that on iron was too low. It introduced, besides, the obnoxious minimum principle, which has been so mischievously extended, and to that extent,

I am constrained in candor to acknowledge, as I wish to disguise nothing, the protective principle was recognized by the Act of 1816."
(Against the Force Bill, by John C. Calhoun, 15 & 16 February 1833).

In the early 1800s, the national government instituted direct taxation, claiming it was for the protective custody of the sovereign States. It's surprising to think that under James Madison's leadership, the federal government would introduce a tax under such a rationale. Additionally, the Tariff Act of 1816 seems questionable in terms of constitutionality, given concerns about its proper apportionment. Any government that installs fear in their legislative directives onto their citizenry, is not a government that you can trust. And to create fiscal tax policies for collection based on a fear is tyrannical.

This Tariff Act showed it was not apportioned correctly among the sovereign States because the national government showed privileged towards the manufactures of Pennsylvania while denying any leniency to the states producing agriculture products.

"I may add that all the Southern States voted with South Carolina in support of the bill: not that they had any interest in manufacturers, but on the ground that they had supported the war, and of course, felt a corresponding obligation to sustain those establishments which had grown up under the encouragement it had incidentally afforded, whilst most of the New England land Members were opposed to the measure, principally, as I believe, on opposite principles."

(Against the Force Bill, by John C. Calhoun, 15 & 16 February 1833).

Regardless, if this bill received popular support, a directive based on fear is a directive that is unconstitutional and disheartening to the minds of federalism.

John C. Calhoun stood for federalism first over populism.

Populism is what kills and destroys a Republic and drags it to the centers of the abyss.

I can see why the sovereign States of the North would disapprove of this Tariff Act of 1816 because quite frankly all the wealth of this republic is in the North. This is one issue that Thomas Jefferson cautioned while discussing the fiscal and tax policies of this American Republic. Taxation by the national government creates inequality, disharmony, privileged and hatred. This is one thing that the gentleman of Virginia tried to warn Alexander Hamilton with his autocratic policies for a central bank.

I wished John C. Calhoun would have seen the dangers of this tariff act installed by the general government of the United States. Because this tariff act was not an indirect tax and should have been labeled as a direct tax and declared unconstitutional.

"You give the central government, an inch of power, they will take a yard."

John C. Calhoun should have raised the necessary emergency sirens regarding this intrusion of the federal government in 1816.

"What course now, I would ask, did it become Carolina to pursue in reference to these demands? Instead of acquiescing in them, because she had acted generously in adjusting the tariff of 1816, she saw, in her generosity on that occasion, additional motives for that firm and decided resistance which she has since made against the system of protection." (Against the Force Bill, by John C. Calhoun, 15 & 16 February 1833).

The path forward for Carolina and other states loyal to the American republic is evident. If an act of Congress is deemed unlawful and unconstitutional, the states retain the power of non-cooperation rather than resorting to violent resistance.

"…she never despaired of relief bill till the passage of the Act of 1828 – that bill of abominations – engendered by avarice and political intrigue. Till then, the question had been, whether the protective system was constitutional and expedient; but after that, she no longer considered the question whether the right of regulating the industry of the States was a reserved or delegated power, but what right a State possesses to defend her reserved powers against the encroachments of the Federal Government: a question on the decision of which value of all the reserved power depends. The passage of the Act of 1828, with all its objectionable features, closed the door of hope through the general government." (Against the Force Bill, by John C. Calhoun, 15 & 16 February 1833).

It is not within the national government's purview to implement protective policies for the States, and certainly not policies rooted in fear. This was evident in the approach taken with the 1816 Tariff Act. Regardless of the challenges posed by the War of 1812, the national Congress lacked the authority to institute such a direct taxation policy on individual or all states.

I wish I could have sought clarification from Calhoun about the specific overreaches of the federal government concerning taxation. Various types of federal infringements exist. While I passionately believe that initiatives towards emancipation and civil rights are not overreaches, I am convinced that overstepping boundaries in direct taxation and other areas are clear violations. Such breaches should be addressed by either the courts or the individual sovereign states.

"It afforded conclusive evidence that no reasonable prospect of relief from Congress could be entertained; yet the near approach of the period of the payment of the public debt, and the elevation of General Jackson to the presidency, still afforded a ray of hope – not so strong, however, as to prevent the State from turning her eyes for final relief to her reserved powers."
(Against the Force Bill, by John C. Calhoun, 15 & 16 February 1833).

When you put faith on the national government to faithfully make you believe that they have no interest in obtaining more power than within their enumerated ones, you are wholly mistaken. There is no sign of relief to regain the state's reserved powers when the central government has decreed unlimited and unconstitutional power. The worse thing yet, is when the sovereign state entity and/or its people condone of these actions.

Then it is hard for the federal government to find relieve of these actions and give back the power to the states.

"But while this active canvass was carried on, which looked to the reserved powers as the final means of redress if all others failed, the State at the same time cherished a hope, as I have already stated, that the election of General Jackson to the presidency would prevent the necessity of a resort to extremities. He was identified with the interests of the staple States; and having the same interest, it was believed that his great popularity – a popularity of the strongest character, as it rested on military services – would enable him, as they hoped, gradually to bring down the system of protection, without shock or injury to any interest. Under these views, the canvass in favor of General Jackson's election to the presidency was carried with great zeal, in conjunction with that active inquiry into the reserved powers of the States on which final reliance was placed." (Against the Force Bill, by John C. Calhoun, 15 & 16 February 1833).

The states, respectively the people, should never entrust anyone with the highest office in our American republic who has a higher popularity rating than the devil himself.

"But little did the people of Carolina dream that the man whom they were thus striving to elevate to the highest seat of power would prove so utterly false to all their hopes." (Against the Force Bill, by John C. Calhoun, 15 & 16 February 1833).

"Man is, indeed, ignorant of the future; nor was there a stronger illustration of the observation than is afforded by the result of that election!" (Against the Force Bill, by John C. Calhoun, 15 & 16 February 1833).

Upon examining Calhoun's remarks, it is evident that he was not swayed by the populist allure often associated with figures like Andrew Jackson. Calhoun recognized the dangers of entrancing political rhetoric that might win votes but lead to decisions the public would later regret, particularly in the form of increased direct taxation by the federal government. As humans, we have the capacity to learn from our past, evolve, and stand against policies that we once might have supported. Calhoun's transformation and eventual opposition to the Tariff Act of

1816 and the overreaching authority of the presidency exemplifies this. He remained steadfast in his principles, siding with Carolina in challenging Jackson's controversial policies. As we saw in 1816, 1832, 1894, 1913, 1935, 1965, 2001, through the present, the national government has wielded its power onto the entity of the sovereign states.

"Has Congress the right to pass this bill?" (Against the Force Bill, by John C. Calhoun, 15 & 16 February 1833).

The Force Bill consisted of the following:

"There is no limitation on the power of the sword; - and that over the purse is equally without restraint; for among the extraordinary features of the bill, it contains no appropriation, which, under existing circumstances, is tantamount to an unlimited appropriation." (Against the Force Bill, by John C. Calhoun, 15 & 16 February 1833).

"The bill violates the Constitution, plainly and palpably, in many of its provisions, by authorizing the President, at his pleasure, to place the different ports of the Union on an unequal footing, contrary to that provision of the

Constitution which declares that no preference shall be given to one port over another. It also violates the Constitution by authorizing him, at his discretion, to impose cash-duties-in one port, while credit is allowed in others, by enabling the President to regulate commerce, a power vested in Congress alone; and by drawing within jurisdiction of the United States courts, powers never intended to be conferred on them." (Against the Force Bill, by John C. Calhoun, 15 & 16 February 1833).

"As great as these objections are, they become insignificant in the provisions of a bill which, by a single blow – by treating the States as a mere lawless mass of individuals – prostrates all the barriers of the Constitution." (Against the Force Bill, by John C. Calhoun, 15 & 16 February 1833).

The presidency of Andrew Jackson, or should we call it to what it really was, the tyranny of Andrew Jackson, was the beginning of a rogue and arrogant federal government. This federal act of Congress, fully sponsored by President Jackson, shows a vast contradiction as to what the powers of the general government has, not only on the issue of taxation but on other issues that are truly vested in the powers of the sovereign states.

"The State has never, it is true, relied upon that tribunal, the Supreme Court, to vindicate its reserved rights; yet they have always considered it an auxiliary means of defense, of which they would gladly have availed themselves to test the constitutionality of protection, had they not been deprived of the means of doing so by the act of the majority."

> The power of nullification is more powerful than the power of the federal government.

(Against the Force Bill, by John C. Calhoun, 15 & 16 February 1833).

This direct federal tax law unfortunately was not passed in 1894, as that law was declared unconstitutional. If the Court, in this case spearheaded by Chief Justice Roger Taney, a friend to the centralization of the federal government, was not going to declare a national direct tax law unconstitutional, then it would be up to the sovereign states to declare it unconstitutional. The power of nullification is more powerful than the power of the federal government.

"The people of Carolina believe that the Union is a union of States, and not of individuals; that it was formed by the States, and that the citizens of the several States were bound to it through the acts of their several States; that each State ratified the Constitution for itself, and that it was only by such ratification of a State that any obligation was imposed upon its citizens." (Against the Force Bill, by John C. Calhoun, 15 & 16 February 1833).

Calhoun and I both share the same sentiment that this republic was established to be a union of (sovereign) States to o be bounded under one common cause, the Constitution.

"Thus, believing, it is the opinion of the people of Carolina that it belongs to the State which has imposed the obligation to declare, in the last resort, the extent of this obligation, as far as her citizens which exist in all analogous cases of compact between sovereign bodies. On this principle the people of the State, acting in their sovereign capacity in convention, precisely as they did in the adoption of their own and the Federal Constitution." (Against the Force Bill, by John C. Calhoun, 15 & 16 February 1833).

Calhoun and I both indeed still share the same sentiment. That the union of states and the general government must respect their boundaries dictated in their own constitutions as well as in the federal Constitution. Both entities must respect one another and keep their powers in check without crossing boundaries.

Indeed, the power of Nullification is more powerful than the might of the federal government. The American citizenry have for the most part forgotten this tool to use within their own sovereign state to put a stop to the intrusive and obtrusive general government of the United States. Our education system, both private and public, have removed this type of studies from our curriculum and instituted a new form of educational indoctrination of Social Studies.

Nullification is a concept rooted deeply in the early years of the United States and reflects the ongoing tensions between state and federal authority. The **Virginia and Kentucky**

Resolutions of 1798, authored anonymously by James Madison and Thomas Jefferson respectively, were in response to the Alien and Sedition Acts passed by the Federalist-controlled Congress in the same year. The concept of nullification was not restricted to one region of the country or to one specific issue. While the Nullification Crisis of the early 1830s was centered in the South over tariffs, the 1850s saw Northern states invoke the principle in response to the Fugitive Slave Act. Calhoun made it possible to present nullification legislation against the federal direct tax of tariffs that President Jackson successfully proposed and made Congress pass into law.

"The very point at issue between the two parties there, is, whether nullification is a peaceable and an efficient remedy against an unconstitutional act of the General Government, and may be asserted as such through the State tribunals."

(Against the Force Bill, by John C. Calhoun, 15 & 16 February 1833).

"Both parties agree that the acts against which it is directed are unconstitutional and oppressive."

(Against the Force Bill, by John C. Calhoun, 15 & 16 February 1833).

Any act of the national government, not deemed to be constitutional, is an act of unconstitutionality and oppressive. Is the act of nullification, an act of peaceable and remedy measure against the federal government? I will let Calhoun answer that question.

"Sir, I consider this bill, and the arguments which have been urged on this floor in its support, as the most triumphant acknowledgement that nullification is peaceful and efficient, and so deeply intrenched in the principles of our system, that it cannot be assailed but by prostrating the Constitution, and substituting the supremacy of military force in lieu of the supremacy of the laws." (Against the Force Bill, by John C. Calhoun, 15 & 16 February 1833).

The peaceful remedy of nullification is more efficient than the violent acts made by John Brown. Violence and counter violence do not solve anything and just create a more hostile environment. The theory of this process is not to gain any power but to claim that power already stated in the Constitution.

"Why, then, do they not leave this controversy to that tribunal? Why do they not confide to them the abrogation of the ordinance, and the laws made in pursuance of it, and the assertion of that supremacy which they claim for the laws of Congress? The State stands pledged to resist no process of the court." (Against the Force Bill, by John C. Calhoun, 15 & 16 February 1833).

If the states confide for a judgment in the courts, especially the Supreme Court, you are surrendering your reserved state sovereignty to the national government. We should never go down this path because it will lead us straight into the autocratic abyss.

Once the state receives the judgment from the courts, the state he has no option but to cease resistance to avoid chaos within our republic. People have the wrong impression of how to handle our reserved rights and they believe that the judiciary is the answer, but nothing could be further from the truth.

"Why, then, confer on the President the extensive and unlimited powers provided in this bill? Why authorize him to use military force to arrest the civil process of the State?" (Against the Force Bill, by John C. Calhoun, 15 & 16 February 1833).

I will let Calhoun answer this question.

"But if the Senator from Virginia means to assert that the twenty-four States form but one community, with a single sovereign power as to the objects of the Union, it will be but the revival of the question of whether the Union is a union between States as distinct communities, or a mere aggregate of the American people as a mass of individuals; and in this light his opinions would lead directly to consolidation. But to return to the bill." (Against the Force Bill, by John C. Calhoun, 15 & 16 February 1833).

"It is said that the bill ought to pass, because the law must be enforced. The law must be enforced! The imperial edict must be executed! It is under such sophistry, couched in general terms, without looking to the limitations which must ever exist in the practical exercise of power, that the most cruel and despotic acts ever have been covered. It was such a sophistry as this that cast

Daniel into the lions' den and the three Innocents into the fiery furnace. Under the same sophistry the bloody edicts of Nero and Caligula were executed. The law must be enforced.

Yes, the act imposing the a "tea-tax must be executed." This was the very argument which impelled Lord North and his administration to the mad career which forever separated us from the British crown. Under a similar sophistry, "that religion must be protected," how many massacres have been perpetrated?" and how many martyrs have been tied to the stake? What! Acting on this vague abstraction, are you prepared to enforce a law without considering whether it be just or unjust, constitutional, or unconstitutional? Will you collect money when it is acknowledged that it is not wanted? He who earns the money, who digs it from the earth with the sweat of his brow, has a right just title to it against the universe.

No one has the right to touch it without consent, except his government, and this only to the extent of its legitimate wants; to take more is robbery, and you propose by this bill to enforce robbery by murder. Yes: to this result you must come by this miserable sophistry, this vague abstraction of enforcing the law, without a regard to the fact whether the law be just or unjust, constitutional, or unconstitutional." (Against the Force Bill, by John C. Calhoun, 15 & 16 February 1833).

The former esteemed senator of South Carolina stated: if a law, decree, or edict is just and constitutional and is to be enforced by a higher power it should only occur if it was never illegal or unconstitutional.

The government has right to commission income from via-taxes but only to the extent to what the constitution tends to favor the legality of the enumerated powers.

In this case, the federal government has no legal means to pass any form of taxation onto the states, especially when it is not apportioned correctly. John C. Calhoun and I have never denied the power of taxation upon the levels of the national government. But we agree their powers are of indirect taxation and by form of tariffs if they are truly apportioned.

But the federal government has never proved quite well how to show their direct taxation of state apportionment, only on theory, but never on reality. The reason why, is it cannot be done and that is why the direct taxation policies are left up to the States, respectively the people. If there was such a bill, regardless of the Sixteenth Amendment, the States, and the people have a right to refuse but it is quite hard for them to do that now because of the next Amendment on the list denying the people's right to refuse a federal taxation act of congress.

I will detail on my next chapters in why the Sixteenth Amendment is sanctioned robbery and the Seventeenth Amendment is denying the sovereign states' refusal to cooperate with such tax policies.

IV.

"The Congress shall have power to lay and collect taxes on incomes, from whatever source derived, without apportionment among the several States, and without regard to any census or enumeration."

Sixteenth Amendment to the
United States Constitution

After the Supreme Court ruled that a federal tax was considered a direct tax, proponents of the tax turned to Justice Harlan's dissenting opinion. Justice Harlan argued that the tax was not direct and, thus, constitutional. He also suggested that if Congress lacked the authority to pass such a law, the Constitution should be amended to allow it. The Constitution, while amendable, is grounded in its original intent. This foundational document ensures a balance of power, with states retaining significant authority. The federal government's powers are explicitly listed, whereas states possess a broader and more varied range of powers. In the realm of taxation, states are vested with the authority to levy direct taxes, whereas the national government holds the power to impose indirect taxes. An amendment granting the federal government the power of direct taxation could be an overreach of states' rights and powers. When these powers are placed in the hands of popularly elected officials, there are concerns about potential misuse. The addition of certain amendments to the Constitution has been controversial. Some argue that allowing the federal government to impose taxes without clear limits or apportionment can be problematic for American citizens. In the end, the Sixteenth Amendment, the power of direct taxation, is best described as sanctioned robbery. Why would the robber ever go back to an illegal life of crime?

This is where I will explain that this amendment is nothing more than a legal form of theft. From 1913 to the present, the federal government has been given that license to steal with no accountability, repercussions, or convictions.

The American people instead of fighting back to reclaim their own state sovereignty by repealing this evil amendment, and the one that came after it, instead ignore what is happening to our republic. They rather see reforms being presented from their congressional delegations, rather than repeals.

The American citizenry rather see a repeal of an amendment to reclaim an old vice, than a repeal of an amendment to reclaim their wallets.

I'm troubled that the American citizenry often wants to fight against a federal government encroachment, but often too late in the game.

Now, let us tell the tale of post-1913 trauma and drama of the federal government's power and legal overreach of our taxation policies. The way the American people ignore rather than act to fight these two amendment encroachments against the states.

The establishments of laws that came after the establishment of the Sixteenth Amendment were all legal and sanctioned by the elusive amendment in question.

"The Income Tax Law of 1913 is not unconstitutional as not conforming with, or being beyond the authority of, the Sixteenth Amendment." (Syllabus of Stanton v. Baltic Mining Company, 1916).

"Section 310(b)(1) of the Tax Equity and Fiscal Responsibility Act of 1982 does not violate the Tenth Amendment or constitutional principles of federalism by effectively compelling States to issue bonds in registered form." (Syllabus of South Carolina v. Baker, Secretary of the Treasury, 1988).

"(a) The Tenth Amendment limits Congress' authority to regulate state activities are structural, not substantive—that is, the States must find their protection from congressional regulation through the national political process, not through judicially defined spheres of unregulated state activity." (Syllabus of South Carolina v. Baker, Secretary of the Treasury, 1988).

The court does not have the authority to overrule an amendment, but states can work to raise awareness and advocate for change through their congressional delegation in Congress. It is up to Congress and the states, through the constitutional amendment process, to address and potentially repeal amendments. It isn't within the judiciary's purview to decide on the validity of an amendment.

In the main syllabus of *South Carolina v. Baker*, 1988, the high court clearly defined the powers of the states and general government of the United States. The limitations of Congress' powers are structural and not substantive, meaning that no one can truly bring a challenge to amendments being part of the Constitution.

"Section 310(b)(1) does not violate the doctrine of intergovernmental tax immunity by taxing the interest earned on unregistered state bonds. Section 310(b)(1) is inconsistent with its Court's holding in *Pollock v. Farmer's Loan & Trust Co.*, 157 U.S. 429, that state bond interest was immune from nondiscriminatory federal tax, but that decision has been effectively overruled by subsequent case law. Under the intergovernmental tax immunity jurisprudence prevailing Pollock's time, neither the Federal nor the State Governments could tax income that an individual directly derived from any contract with the other government." (Syllabus of South Carolina v. Baker, Secretary of the Treasury, 1988).

"The Income Tax Law, as applied to mining companies, directly taxes a portion of their principal or capital, without apportionment according to population, and, therefore is unconstitutional. Direct taxes on principal or capital, not being taxes on income, are not authorized by the Sixteenth Amendment." (Appellant Argument or Mr. Charles A. Snow of Stanton v. Baltic Mining Company, 1916).

But sadly, Since the passage of the Sixteenth Amendment, there has been a significant increase in direct tax legislation from the national government. This has led to increased spending on various projects, from national infrastructure to foreign aid. Some constitutional scholars argue that the federal government's actions go beyond what was intended by the Sixteenth Amendment. "(1) That as the Sixteenth Amendment authorizes only an exceptional direct income tax without apportionment, to which the tax in question does not conform, it is therefore not within the authority of the Sixteenth Amendment." (Opinion of the Court of Stanton v. Baltic Mining Company by Chief Justice Edward D. White, 1916).

"(2) Not being within the authority of the Sixteenth Amendment the tax is therefore, within the ruling of *Pollock v. Farmer's Loan & Trust Co.,* 157 U.S. 429; 158 U.S. 601, a direct tax and void for want of compliance with the regulation of apportionment." (Opinion of the Court of Stanton v. Baltic Mining Company by Chief Justice Edward D. White, 1916).

"But this merely asserts a right to take the taxation of mining corporations out of the rule established by the Sixteenth Amendment when there is no authority for so doing." (Opinion of the Court of Stanton v. Baltic Mining Company by Chief Justice Edward D. White, 1916).

This case and the *Brushaber* case enter a valid constitutional legality point.

The Constitution grants the government specific powers, and neither sovereign states nor individuals can challenge a law based solely on disagreement. To address grievances with a law or amendment, the appropriate response is to seek its repeal, not merely its reform. Many believe that efforts to reform the tax structure may only embolden the federal government, rather than limit its reach. As such, some argue that the best course of action is to advocate for repeal. Reforming the tax structure will only increase the arrogance of the federal government. "But aside from the obvious error of the proposition intrinsically considered, it manifestly disregards the fact that by the previous ruling it was settled that the provisions of the Sixteenth Amendment conferred no new power of taxation but simply prohibited the previous complete and plenary power of income taxation possessed by Congress from the beginning from being taken out of category of indirect taxation to which inherently belonged and being placed in the category of direct taxation subject to apportionment by a consideration of the sources from which the income was derived, that is by testing the tax not by what it was—a tax on income, but by a mistake theory deduced from the origin or source of the income taxed." (Opinion of the Court of Stanton v. Baltic Mining Company by Chief Justice Edward D. White, 1916).

Chief Justice Edward White makes a powerful claim that this republic was no stranger to the power of taxation. Prior to the Sixteenth Amendment, the national government had the power of taxation, indirect taxation. The hint of a national direct taxation never came to play because the national government had to proportion its taxation among the sovereign states. In both theory and practice, this apportionment proved challenging to implement. Many taxation policies, which did not adhere to apportioned federal direct taxation, went unchecked. This was a key reason Calhoun strongly opposed the 1832 tariffs. In 1894, American jurisprudence stepped in and declared a federal direct tax law unconstitutional. However, this decision paved the way for proponents to seek its legalization through a constitutional amendment. With the introduction of this amendment, every time the Congress opens its session doors, or a president is inaugurated, new sanctioned robbery is forced onto the States and its citizens.

The congressional terms after 1913, and presidential terms of Herbert Hoover, Franklin

D. Roosevelt, Harry S. Truman, Dwight D. Eisenhower, John F. Kennedy, Lyndon B. Johnson, Richard Nixon, Gerald Ford, Jimmy Carter, Ronald Reagan, George HW Bush, Bill Clinton, George W. Bush, Barack H. Obama, Donald J. Trump, and now Joseph Biden, have shown us outrageous and unrestrained forms of direct taxation.

The New Deal policies under Roosevelt brought nothing but unrestrained and unapportion direct taxation until this very day, affecting the lives of many citizens of the states. The infrastructure form of unrestrained taxation and spending from the Eisenhower policies have led to a totalitarian invasive control over our sovereign states' commerce under the sanctioned robbery legality that is the Sixteenth Amendment and illegal induction into the Commerce Clause. The Great Society policies of Lyndon Baines Johnson extended the rule of taxation to new levels to include social program taxation and spending.

And this continues to this very day.

The American people need to focus their attention on repeal, rather than reform. Reform has not and will not fix our republic but will simply complicate and entice it to pursue more robberies to add to the coffers of the Federal Treasury.

Even today, the national Congress has passed multiple forms of direct taxation unapportioned and unrestrained across the sovereign states. Education fiscal spending known as the 2001 No Child Left Behind Act under President George W. Bush. And now the national Congress just approved $4.2 billion to give to the State of California, unapportionable, for the so-called construction of a bullet train from Los Angeles to San Francisco. But that bullet train idea did not stop in California, there were unprincipled unapportion taxation and spending in a bullet train from Springfield, IL., to Chicago, IL. In 2009, President Obama signed the Affordable Care Act, which signaled a blow of unapportioned and unrestrained taxation and spending on the healthcare status of all citizens of the states.

The question of apportionment continues to be a concern today, as evidenced by recent legislation such as the Pact Act. This legislation is designed to address the healthcare needs of veterans affected by toxins and chemicals during their service in Iraq and Afghanistan. A pressing question remains: how will these funds be distributed? The distribution of funds for veterans from the Pact Act raises questions about which states, and which veterans will benefit. Critics argue that the federal government may be showing favoritism, lacking clear apportionment. While such actions may be within the bounds of the Sixteenth Amendment, concerns about fairness and principle persist. Why do people not express outrage about how the national government continues to act since 1913? The Constitution has granted access to open the Treasury coffers. With no regulatory observance, the general government has continued to do what they have been granted permission to do since 1913. The people, instead of repealing this vile Sixteenth Amendment, just whine and ask for more dependent welfare income or menial reforms.

We all understand that the government of all nations needs funds from its citizens or corporations. But this is a special nation that has a special form of government. The relationship between state and federal government in the United States, particularly in the realm of taxation, has been a complex and evolving one. Historically, the Constitution sought to strike a balance between state and federal powers. We did not need to pass an amendment stating the obvious.

If the Sixteenth Amendment would have never come to pass, all these federal tax laws would have been declared a direct tax and unconstitutional. We would not have had uninformed American citizens seeking to challenge laws that unfortunately have a sanctioned legality within the Constitution.

Three years after the Sixteenth Amendment was passed by the national Congress and then ratified by the sovereign states, two cases were taken to the high court to challenge the constitutionality of this amendment.

The high court regrettably but reasonably sided with the Constitution and the amendment in question.

"But this merely asserts a right to take the taxation of mining corporations out of the rule established by the Sixteenth Amendment when there is no authority for so doing." (Opinion of the Court of Stanton v. Baltic Mining Company by Chief Justice Edward D. White, 1916).

The Supreme Court is a funny institution. Whereas the justices find constitutionality in a federal direct tax law and yet cannot find constitutionality in a sovereign state naturalization enforcement case. Both are constitutional.

"We say wholly fallacious assumption because independently of the effect of the operation of the Sixteenth Amendment it was settled in *Stratton's Independence v. Howbert*, 231 U.S. 399, that such a tax is not a tax upon the property as such because of its ownership, but a true excise levied on the results of the business of carrying on mining corporations (pp.413 *et seq.*)" (Opinion of the Court of Stanton v. Baltic Mining Company by Chief Justice Edward D. White, 1916).

In the United States, before the ratification of the Sixteenth Amendment in 1913, direct tax laws proposed by the federal government would likely have faced significant constitutional challenges. This amendment provided Congress the power to levy income taxes without distributing them among the states based on population.

Similarly, the Seventeenth Amendment, ratified in the same year, allowed for the direct election of Senators by the voters of each state. Prior to this, Senators were chosen by state legislatures.

Both amendments signified significant shifts in the balance of state and federal powers. While reforms to policies or laws can be addressed through the legislative process, reversing the impact of a constitutional amendment requires its repeal, a substantial effort demanding broad consensus in both Congress and among the states.

And yet, we, as an American republic of sovereign States and its citizens of the United States have not seen yet fit to be rid of such an unprincipled amendment.

In the 69 years since the ratification of the Sixteenth Amendment, it has been a point of contention for many, but it remains part of the Constitution. Critics argue that the amendment has provided the federal government with unchecked authority over taxation, calling it unprincipled. Despite the concerns, the Sixteenth Amendment remains a cornerstone of the federal government's taxation powers.

* * *

"Congress was not empowered by the Sixteenth Amendment to tax, as income of the stockholder, without apportionment, a stock dividend made lawfully and in good faith against profits accumulated by the corporation since March 1, 1913. *Towne v. Eisner*, 245 U.S. 418." (Syllabus of the Court of Eisner, As Collector of United States Internal Revenue for the Third District of the State of New York v. Macomber, 1920).

"This case presents the question whether, by virtue of the Sixteenth Amendment, Congress has the power to tax, as income of the stockholder and without apportionment, a stock dividend made lawfully and in good faith against profits accumulated by the corporation since March 1, 1913. It arises under the Revenue Act of September 8, 1916, c. 463, 39 Stat. 756, et seq., which in our opinion (notwithstanding a contention of the Government that will be noticed), plainly evinces the purpose of Congress to tax dividends as income." (Opinion of the Court of Eisner, As Collector of United States Internal Revenue for the Third District of the State of New York v. Macomber by Associate Justice Mahlon Pitney, 1920).

I am going to skip the semantics of the opinion in detailing the story of the case. I am going to go into how and why the high court of this land dictated that a stock dividend is not income. Therefore, need not be applied by the Sixteenth Amendment.

If a stock dividend is not considered an income by the court, what else can be considered not income, and not be taxed? Gas? Food? Lodging? Where does gas, food, lodging taxes apply to be apportioned? Are they going to apportion it from my car as I use it on state and county roads? Are they going to apportion it from my stomach as my food is being digested? Are they going to apportion it from my pillow as I wake up from a night at a Holiday Inn? All these taxes should be considered unconstitutional as is the stock dividend. Because if the court ruled that a stock dividend is not a source of income, then the taxation of those items should be unconstitutional as well.

It is the federal government playing the Privilege Under Law came, allowing their special interests to supersede the interests of the Constitution.

"She [Defendant] was called upon to pay, and did under protest, tax imposed under the Revenue Act of 1916, based upon a supposed income of $19,877 because of the new shares; and an appeal to the Commissioner of Internal Revenue having disallowed, she brought action against the Collector to recover the tax. In her complaint she alleged the above facts, and contended that in imposing such a tax the Revenue Act of 1916 violated Art. I, Section 2, cl. 3, and Art. I, Section 9, cl. 4, of the Constitution of the United States, requiring direct taxes to be apportioned according to population, and that the stock dividend was not income within the meaning of the Sixteenth Amendment." (Opinion of the Court of Eisner, As Collector of United States Internal Revenue for the Third District of the State of New York v. Macomber by Associate Justice Mahlon Pitney, 1920).

Truly, how is income defined by law? How is it that the national government gets to define what is an income and what is not an income? How is that the national government defines this instead of the states?

The defendant in this case, feels the anxiety of having to pay a tax on the "income" or better to say the "money" she worked to obtain. And she will do everything in her power to maintain it without having the government take it away from her.

But it is sad to see the federal government, high court, twist the Constitution and disavow its meaning to play privilege politics. For the high court to play privilege politics, they are presenting a position of mistrust against the states and the people.

"Congress was at liberty under the Amendment to tax as income, without apportionment, everything that became income, in the ordinary sense of the word, after the adoption of the Amendment, including dividends received in the ordinary course by a stockholder from a corporation, even though they were extraordinary in amount and might appear upon analysis to be a mere realization in possession of an inchoate and contingent that the stock holder had in surplus of corporate assets previously existing. In *Peabody v. Eisner* (pp. 349-350), we observed that the decision of the District Court in *Towne v. Eisner* had been reversed "only upon the ground that it related to a stock dividend which in fact took nothing from the property of the corporation and added nothing to the interest of the shareholder, but merely changed the evidence which represented that interest;" and we distinguished the *Peabody Case* from the *Towne Case* upon the ground that "the *Peabody Case* from the *Towne Case* upon ground that "the dividend of Baltimore & Ohio shares was not a stock dividend but a distribution *in specie* of a portion of the assets of the Union Pacific." (Opinion of the Court of Eisner, As Collector of United States Internal Revenue for the Third District of the State of New York v. Macomber by Associate Justice Mahlon Pitney, 1920).

"Congress cannot by any definition it may adopt conclude the matter, since it cannot by legislation alter the Constitution, from which alone it derives its power to legislate, and within whose limitations alone that power can be lawfully exercised." (Opinion of the Court of Eisner, As Collector of United States Internal Revenue for the Third District of the State of New York v. Macomber by Associate Justice Mahlon Pitney, 1920).

"Nevertheless, in view of the importance of the matter, and the fact that Congress in the Revenue Act of 1916 declared (39 Stat. 757) that a "stock dividend shall be considered income, to the amount of its cash value," we will deal at length with the constitutional question, incidentally testing the soundness of our previous conclusion." (Opinion of the Court of Eisner, As Collector of United States Internal Revenue for the Third District of the State of New York v. Macomber by Associate Justice Mahlon Pitney, 1920).

No one here is denying the rights that Congress must present laws to the republic that are constitutionally acceptable. And I truthfully see nothing wrong with the Revenue Act of 1916, passed by Congress. This act may very well be constitutionally acceptable, but it is not principledly acceptable. Just because something is legal does not necessarily mean it is viewed as morally or ethically right by everyone. It is a nuance that is important in many policy debates.

I truly see no reason to undeclare a stock dividend by the Court as taxable income. People must realize that any source of income taken by the government is willfully considered a tax. Whether it is a gas, food, telecommunications, travel, or lodging tax, it is still income taken out of your pocket and into the pockets of the national government. A stock dividend is no different than those items, and the high court is condoning a privilege under law to that effect.

"The Sixteenth Amendment must be construed in connection with the taxing clauses of the original Constitution and the effect attributed to them before the Amendment was adopted. In *Pollock v. Farmers' Loan & Trust Co.*, 158 U.S. 601, under the Act of August 27, 1894, c. 349, Section 27, 28 Stat. 509, 553, it was held that taxes upon rents and profits of real estate and upon returns from investments of personal property were in effect direct taxes upon the property from which such income arose, imposed by reason of ownership; and that Congress could not impose such taxes without apportioning them among the States according to population, as required by Art. 1, section 2, cl. 3, and section 9, cl. 4, of the original Constitution." (Opinion of the Court of Eisner, As Collector of United States Internal Revenue for the Third District of the State of New York v. Macomber by Associate Justice Mahlon Pitney, 1920).

"Afterwards, and evidently in recognition of the limitation upon the taxing power of Congress thus determined, the Sixteenth Amendment was adopted, in words lucidly expressing the object to be accomplished: **"The Congress shall have the power to lay and collect taxes on incomes, from whatever source derived, without apportionment among the several States, and without regard to any census or enumeration."** As repeatedly held, this did not extend the taxing power to new subjects, but merely removed the necessity which otherwise might exist for an apportionment among the States of taxes laid on income. *Brushaber v. Union Pacific R. R. Co.,* 240 U.S. 1, 17-19; *Stanton v. Baltic Mining Co.,* 240 U.S. 103, 112 *et seq.*; *Peck & Co. V. Lowe,* 247 U.S. 165, 172-173."
(Opinion of the Court of Eisner, As Collector of United States Internal Revenue for the Third District of the State of New York v. Macomber by Associate Justice Mahlon Pitney, 1920).

"The Sixteenth Amendment proclaimed February 25, 1913, declares: ""The Congress shall have the power to lay and collect taxes on incomes, from whatever source derived, without apportionment among the several States, and without regard to any census or enumeration." (Dissenting Opinion of Eisner, As Collector of United States Internal Revenue for the Third District of the State of New York v. Macomber by Associate Justice Louis Brandeis, 1920).

"The Revenue Act of September 8, 1916, c. 463, 39 Stat. 756, 757, provided: "That the term 'dividends' as used in this title shall be held to mean any distribution made or ordered to be made by a corporation, … out of its earnings or profits accrued since March first, nineteen hundred and thirteen, and payable to its shareholders, whether in cash or stock of the corporation … which stock dividend shall be considered income, to the amount of its cash value." (Dissenting Opinion of Eisner, As Collector of United States Internal Revenue for the Third District of the State of New York v. Macomber by Associate Justice Louis Brandeis, 1920).

To me, the language of this amendment is quite clear. I am not sure why the court was split and not following the letter of this Amendment as it is currently written.

The language is quite clear. "From whatever source derived, the Congress shall have the power to lay and collect taxes on income."

Pollock was a decision made in 1895, whether Congress did not have the Constitutional power to lay and collect any direct tax on income from whatever source derived. The *Pollock* decision was partly superseded by the Sixteenth Amendment. To the eyes of the federal government, there is no partly or full decision especially when the Amendment's language states quite clearly "from whatever source derived."

Thank God, dear readers, I am not a politician so I can speak frankly and succinctly on the political, economic, and social matters of this republic. In 1895, the Supreme Court ruled that the federal income tax was unconstitutional unless apportioned among the states. However, this decision was effectively overturned by the ratification of the Sixteenth Amendment in 1913. Despite this change, in 1920, the court found that stock dividends were not taxable income, maintaining that they did not represent a realized gain.

So, we can truly make a case that gas, food, lodging, telecommunications, and air travel are not income and therefore should not be taxed – as well as personal and professional income. If the court can find privilege in stock dividends, then they must find privilege in these other items. And therefore, for the first time in American history decide that a constitutional amendment is in fact, unconstitutional.

If the court can find one source of income not to be a taxable source of income, then it leaves the case open to re-examine the language of the amendment.

The court might ask Congress to reconsider the amendment's wording for potential modification or repeal. I lean toward repeal. Let's compare both viewpoints on the amendment's phrasing to determine if Congress needs to address its clarity. "The fundamental relation of "capital" to "income" has been discussed by economists, the former being likened to the tree or the land, the latter to the fruit or the crop; the former depicted as a reservoir supplied from springs, the latter as the outlet stream, to be measured by its flow during a period of time. For the present purpose we require only a clear definition of the term "income", as used in common speech, in order to determine its meaning of the Amendment; and having formed also a correct judgment as to the nature of a stock dividend, we shall find it easy to decide the matter at issue." (Opinion of the Court of Eisner, As Collector of United States Internal Revenue for the Third District of the State of New York v. Macomber by Associate Justice Mahlon Pitney, 1920).

"Brief as it is, it indicates the characteristic and distinguishing attribute of income essential for a correct solution of the present controversy. The Government, although basing its argument upon the definition as quoted, placed chief emphasis upon the word :gain," which was extended to include a variety of meanings; while the significance of the next three words was either overlooked or misconceived. *"Derived—from—capital"*; — *"the gain—derived—from—capital,"* etc." "The same fundamental conception is clearly set forth in the

Sixteenth Amendment—"incomes, from whatever source derived"—the essential thought being expressed with a conciseness and lucidity entirely in harmony with the form and style of the Constitution." (Opinion of the Court of Eisner, As Collector of United States Internal Revenue for the Third District of the State of New York v. Macomber by Associate Justice Mahlon Pitney, 1920).

"Can a stock dividend, considering its essential character, be brought within the definition? We refer, of course, to a corporation such as the one in the case at bar, organized for profit, and having a capitol stock divided into shares to which a nominal or par value is attributed." (Opinion of the Court of Eisner, As Collector of United States Internal Revenue for the Third District of the State of New York v. Macomber by Associate Justice Mahlon Pitney, 1920).

"Is there anything in the phraseology of the Sixteenth Amendment or in the nature of corporate dividends which should lead to a departure from these rules of construction and compel this Court to hold, that Congress is powerless to prevent a result so extraordinary as that here contended for by the stockholder?" (Dissenting Opinion of Eisner, As

Collector of United States Internal Revenue for the Third District of the State of New York v. Macomber by Associate Justice Louis Brandeis, 1920).

"First, the term "income" when applied to the investment of the stockholder in a corporation, had, before the adoption of the Sixteenth Amendment, been commonly understood to mean the returns from time to time received by the stockholder from gains or earnings of the corporation. A dividend received by a stockholder from a corporation may be either in distribution of capital assets or in distribution of profits. Whether it is one or the other is in no way affected by the medium in which it is paid, nor by the method or means through which the particular thing is distributed as a dividend was procured." (Dissenting Opinion of Eisner, As Collector of United States Internal Revenue for the Third District of the State of New York v. Macomber by Associate Justice Louis Brandeis, 1920).

As the Court decides to rewrite an act of Congress, to find a way to prove its unconstitutionality. They are rewriting away their own form of unconstitutionality.

Capital is income and income is capital, regardless of how you put it. *"Derived—from—capital—is—income—and—need—to—be–taxed"*; — *"the gain—derived—from—capital—is—income—and—need—to—be—taxed."* All sources of income generated by a citizen, unfortunately, are considered income and must be taxed in accordance with the Sixteenth Amendment. Despite my aversion to this amendment, I find myself in agreement with the court's dissenting opinion. I never thought I, as a strict constitutionalist, would side with Justice Brandeis. The Court, that day, seemed to interpret the law differently rather than applying it based on the Sixteenth Amendment. It ventured into a territory that traditionally belongs to Congress, setting a concerning precedent. The language of the Amendment hasn't changed, and it shouldn't be altered to cater to the Court's preferences. As I've mentioned before, the Court seemed to prioritize 'Privilege Under Law' over 'Equality Under Law.' They appeared to grant advantages to specific citizens with higher incomes, exempting them from certain taxes. The legislative branch of the federal government pushed for this Amendment, mainly because a previous court had invalidated a congressional act lacking constitutional support. However, now with the Constitution on its side, the Court seems eager to reinterpret it based on its interests. Based on the Amendment's wording, Congress has the power to tax any income earned by citizens. Though I am a strict constitutionalist and strongly disagree with the passage of this amendment, I believe it is essential to adhere to its exact language. It is up to Congress to decide whether to adjust its terms or remove it from the Constitution, not the Court's. Associate Justice Oliver Wendell Holmes might benefit from a closer reading of the Constitution. In later years, he denied a citizen her due process rights, allowing Virginia to make a significant decision about her personal rights. However, let us consider his stance on taxation.

"I think that Towne v. Eisner, 245 U.S. 418, was right in its reasoning and result and that on sound principles the stock dividend was not income. But it was clearly intimidated in that case that the construction of the statute then before the Court might be different from that of the Constitution. 245 U.S. 425. I think that the word "incomes" in the Sixteenth Amendment should be read in " a sense most obvious to the common understanding at the time of its adoption." Bishop v. State, 149 Indiana, 223, 230; State v. Butler, 70 Florida, 102, 133. For it was public adoption that it was proposed. *McCollough v. Maryland*, 4 Wheat. 316, 407. The known purpose of this Amendment was to get rid of nice questions as to what direct taxes might be, and I cannot doubt that most people not lawyers would suppose when they voted for it that they put a question like the present to rest. I am of opinion that the Amendment justifies the tax. See Tax Commissioner v. Putnam, 227 Massachusetts, 522, 532, 533." (Dissenting Opinion of Eisner, As Collector of United States Internal Revenue for the Third District of the State of New York v. Macomber by Associate Justice Oliver Wendell Holmes, 1920).

In the matter of taxation and the current wording of the Amendment, it's clear to me that the act aligns with the Amendment. Justice Holmes introduces the idea of "common sense" to both the Court and the public. Unfortunately, most state legislatures, representing the people, approved the Amendment's language for ratification. It's troubling when attorneys reinterpret the Amendment's language, leading the Court to set a certain precedent, affecting our principles of federalism. Thus, while Justice Holmes may dissent on the taxation issue, he did not uphold the equal protection rights of female citizens.

If Justice Holmes can identify inconsistencies in the Court's interpretation of the Sixteenth Amendment, why couldn't he detect flaws in the Eugenical Sterilization Act of 1924 and dissent appropriately? This highlights an inconsistency in our judicial procedures, reminding us that Supreme Court justices are human first, not just instruments of the law. I do not harbor resentment toward any of the amendments. My intention is not to compare the Fourteenth and Sixteenth Amendments. On a related note, I believe the federal government acknowledged that we are all citizens of the Republic through the Fourteenth, though it doesn't provide them control over immigration and naturalization. The amendment ensures equal treatment under the law, aligning with the equal protection clause. Conversely, the Sixteenth Amendment challenges our federalism principle. The clarity of its language mirrors that of the Fourteenth.

I appreciate that Justice Holmes dissented on the Sixteenth Amendment's misinterpretation but am disheartened by his acceptance of a state act that contradicts the Fourteenth. Both Justices Holmes and Brandeis reference Chief Justice John Marshall in their opinions. I mention this because Marshall, like President Adams, did not fully embody federalism principles. Holmes cites one of Marshall's decisions, while Brandeis quotes him.

"To hold now that earnings both made and paid out after the adoption of the Sixteenth

Amendment cannot be taxed as income of the stockholder, if paid in the form of a stock dividend, involves an exceeding narrow construction of it. As said by Chief Justice Marshall in *Brown v. Maryland*, 12 Wheat. 419, 446: "To construe the power so as to impair its efficacy, would tend to defeat an object, in the attainment of which the American public took, and justly took, that strong interest which arose from a full conviction of its necessity."

In the case Justice Brandeis references, Maryland's statute allowed the state to collect duties from exports entering its harbors. As noted from the Pollock opinion, state taxation policies should be direct, while the federal government handles indirect taxation.

Before 1913, the federal government prioritized its role in indirect taxation through tariffs. This approach was in line with the Constitution. Hence, the 1827 decision in Brown v. Maryland aptly interpreted the Republic's balanced taxation powers between the general government and the states.

However, the Sixteenth Amendment shifted this balance, granting the federal government control over both direct and indirect taxation. The amendment's phrase "from whatever source derived" underscores the broad and unrestrained reach of federal tax powers.

"Thus, from every point of view, we are brought irresistibly to the conclusion that neither under the Sixteenth Amendment nor otherwise has Congress power to tax without apportionment a true stock dividend made lawfully and in good faith, or the accumulated profits behind it, as income of the stockholder. The Revenue Act of 1916, in so far as it imposes a tax upon the stockholder because of such a dividend, contravenes the provisions of Article I, section 2, cl. 3, and Article I, section 9, cl. 4, of the Constitution, and to this extend is invalid notwithstanding the Sixteenth Amendment."

(Opinion of the Court of Eisner, As Collector of United States Internal Revenue for the Third District of the State of New York v. Macomber by Associate Justice Mahlon Pitney, 1920).

"It seems to me clear, therefore, that Congress possesses the power which it exercised to make dividends representing profits, taxable as income, whether the medium in which the dividend is paid be cash or stock, and that it may define, as it has done, what dividends representing profits shall be deemed income. It surely is not clear that the enactment exceeds the power granted by the Sixteenth Amendment. And, as this court has so often said, the high prerogative of declaring an act of Congress invalid, should never be exercised except in a clear case." (Dissenting Opinion of Eisner, As Collector of United States Internal Revenue for the Third District of the State of New York v. Macomber by Associate Justice Oliver Wendell Holmes, 1920).

"It is but a decent respect due to the wisdom, the integrity and the patriotism of the legislative body, by which any law is passed, to presume in favor of its validity, until its violation of the Constitution is proved beyond all reasonable doubt." (Opinion of the Court of Ogden v. Saunders, 1827).

It is clear to me, that the opinion of this court is favoring Article I over the Sixteenth

Amendment, which is somewhat all right to set it, but it is not clearly justified.

The Sixteenth Amendment has established a more justified precedent. I believe that the inclusion of the phrase "from whatever source derived" in the Amendment's language provides clear and broad authority to Congress to levy and collect taxes on various sources of income, including stock dividends, as well as items like gas, food, lodging, telecommunications, and air travel.

The Revenue Act of 1916 aligns with the language and intent of the Amendment, and it is, in my view, entirely justified. However, it is regrettable that the Court chose to disregard this alignment and instead issued its own interpretation. While I am not personally supportive of the Amendment, if it is indeed a part of the Constitution, then it should be respected and applied down to the very last word of its definition.

I choose to stand with the Constitution rather than with the Court. I stand for the clear language of all the Amendments rather than a cheap interpretation of the Court. This constitutional interpretation of the Revenue Act of 1916 is an interpretation of special interests than the interests of the Constitution and the rules of federalism.

I reiterate once more that while the Sixteenth Amendment may be a part of the Constitution and therefore must be respected, it continues to be, in my opinion, unprincipled, both in its inception and as it stands today.

* * *

When the Sixteenth Amendment was ratified, the National Congress enacted the Revenue Act of 1913. While this act imposed an unapportion form of direct taxation, it was legally permissible under the unprincipled amendment in question. In my opinion, there is no doubt that this law was more constitutional than the one that followed in 1935.

There is nothing more questionable and dishonest than for the national government, whether it be Congress or the high court, to erroneously classify a law as a direct tax when it is evidently a fee for a government service and not a tax.

The national Social Security Act of 1935 was initially presented to the sovereign States and their citizens as a fee for a federal program on retiree services. However, it's important to note that national fees are unconstitutional as they are not mentioned in the Constitution. When challenged for its constitutionality, the progressive administration of FDR argued before the high court that this act was a direct tax rather than a fee. Unfortunately, the national high court of the land, in another controversial ruling, deemed this act as a tax. This tax continues to be sanctioned by the Sixteenth Amendment, which many consider to be a legal means of government revenue collection, but others see as a form of legalized robbery.

"The Social Security Act (Act of August 14, 1935, c. 531, 49 Stat. 620, 42 U.S. C., c. 7, (Supp.)) is challenged once again." (Opinion of the Court on Helvering v. Davis, 1937 by Associate Justice Benjamin Cardozo).

"In *Steward Machine Co., v. Davis*, decided this day, ante, p. 548, we have upheld the validity of Title IX of the act, imposing an excise upon employers of eight or more. In this cases Titles VIII and II are the subject of attack. Title VIII lays another excise upon employers in addition to the one imposed by Title IX (though with different exemptions), It lays a special income tax upon employees to be deducted from their wages and paid by the employers. Title II provides for the payment of Old Age Benefits, and supplies the motive and occasion, in the view of the assailants of the statute, for the levy of the taxes imposed by Title VIII. The plan of the two titles will now be summarized more fully." (Opinion of the Court on Helvering v. Davis, 1917 by Associate Justice Benjamin Cardozo).

Title VIII, as we have said, lays two different types of tax, an "income tax on employees," and "an excise tax on employers." (Opinion of the Court on Helvering v. Davis, 1937 by Associate Justice Benjamin Cardozo).

Even with the Sixteenth Amendment, do you believe the federal government has that strict authority and assurance that they can create tax policy on employees' and employers' hard-earned money? They did challenge on that issue and the high court sided once more with the national government.

Whether the national government hatches a plan to pass a national directive with the promise of a retirement safety net, national security protection, or safety infrastructure planning for the nation. It's all faux pretense to commit robbery against the sovereign states under that Sixteenth Amendment scam.

The federal government has no responsibility, nor power to establish these plans. Since 1817, President James Madison, our distinguished Father of the Constitution, vetoed a national bill to increase spending for infrastructure spending across our republic. With a Sixteenth Amendment, or not, the general government of the United States was never intended to be the central of authority for the states.

That authority was left to the states at their discretion and cooperation with one another to make a more perfect union of sovereign states.

"There are penalties for non-payment, Section 807 (c)." (Opinion of the Court on Helvering v. Davis, 1937 by Associate Justice Benjamin Cardozo).

A penalty for non-payment of a tax? That sounds like a fee charge. The federal government does not see the citizen, as a citizen but as a cash cow with the hint of an imagination of indispensable income through taxation.

This is what you get, when the federal government obtains power and launches on an endless tirade for more power and institutionalizing fees as penalties as taxes. Instead of being a support system for the citizen, it is the federal government being a burden to the citizen.

"This suit is brought by a shareholder of the Edison Electric Illuminating Company of Boston, a Massachusetts corporation, to restrain the corporation from making the payments and deductions called for by the act, which is stated to be void under the Constitution of the United States. The bill tells us that the corporation has decided to obey the statute, that it has reached this decision in the face of the complainant's protests, and that it will make the payments and deductions unless restrained by a decree." (Opinion of the Court on Helvering v. Davis, 1937 by Associate Justice Benjamin Cardozo).

Some may say that the income collection of the general government from whatever source they derive it from us, has reached its limits of its constitutional decree. The collection of a Social Security is not a collection of income but an excuse for what really has been concocted to be as robbery.

We all understand the thinking of Justice Cardozo and all the court regarding this decision. But you must really think long and hard before you inflict more financial burden onto the states and its citizens. Yes, there is a national constitutional amendment authorizing the general government and several sovereign States, the right to pass unapportion taxation, but there are limits to everything and this is one of them.

The branches of the federal government are not going to issue a legislative or executive decree to ease a taxation policy that is derived from the Sixteenth Amendment.

"The expected consequences are indicated substantially as follows: The deductions from the wages of the employees will produce unrest among them, and will be followed, it is predicted, by demands that wages be increased. If the exactions shall ultimately be held void, the company will have parted with moneys which as a practical matter it will be impossible to recover. Nothing is said in the bill about the premise of indemnity. The prediction is made also that serious consequences will sue if there is a submission to the excise. The corporation and its shareholders will suffer irreparable loss, and many thousands of dollars will be subtracted from the value of the shares. The prayer is for an injunction and for a declaration that the act is void." (Opinion of the Court on Helvering v. Davis, 1937 by Associate Justice Benjamin Cardozo).

Why would there be a promise of indemnity if that is never the case from a rogue and arrogant federal government. Consequences of this bill is that the employer is forced to deduct from its employees' salaries, a tax or fee, or whatever you want to call it. And the audacity of the general government is to demand to these employers to raise their salaries. It is an oxymoron of poetic political philosophy. The government seeks to collect income from employees' and yet demands that the employer continuously raises their salaries.

This is the progressive way of thinking of making money. Let other people make it, and we collect it. I understand the sanctioned decree in the Constitution, but again, there are limits to that legal decree. To take income out of a so-called Social Security Act as a direct tax is stretching these boundaries of federalism and entering the realm of a centralized autocracy.

Associate Justice Benjamin Cardozo, appointed by Herbert Hoover, is yet another member of American Progressivism, that have ruined, and it continues to ruin our glorious American Republic of sovereign States. To seek prayer to end this law through an injunction or act of Congress is giving false hopes to the states.

The true prayer to void this Act is to bring an end through repeal to the vile sanctioned robbery amendment decree. To bring economic, social stability among the states. You cannot have peaceful economic and social stability when you have a meddling national government dictating fiscal and taxation policies, unapportion to the states and expect all too well and normal. At least, this is not how this republic was established to be and function.

"The scheme of benefits created by the provisions of Title II is not in contravention of the limitations of the Tenth Amendment. Congress may spend money in aid of the "general welfare." Constitution, Art. I, section 8; *United States v. Butler*, 297 U.S. 1, 65; *Steward Machine Co. v. Davis, supra.* (Opinion of the Court on Helvering v. Davis, 1937 by Associate Justice Benjamin Cardozo).

"...to pay the Debts and provide for the common defence and general welfare of the United States; but all Duties, Imposts and Excises shall be uniform throughout the United States." Art. I, section 8; United States Constitution.

Incidentally, does the Sixteenth Amendment stomp over the Tenth Amendment?

Progressives have loved to twist and turn the General Welfare Clause of the Constitution. They truly are sought to believe that it is the general government the one that supplies that base of support.

What is for the protection of the general welfare of the United States? Does it mean to build and regulate the roads, railway, airport, canals, schooling, labor?

No!

The general government of the United States means to institute policy for the protection outside of the realm of its sovereign States. It is the sovereign States that must retain its sovereignty, even in the matters of fiscal, infrastructure and tax policy. The high court instituted a false policy onto the enumerated powers of the federal government.

In *United States v. Butler*, they overturned an act of Congress but not the constitutional decree that gave that power to the act. The

Court was wise not to act legislatively and re-peal the amendment. They just overturned a law and creating the *Stare Decisis* doctrine. It is the Congress, who amends, repeals the Constitution.

The power to amend the Constitution belongs to Congress, which can propose amendments with a two-thirds majority in both the House of Representatives and the Senate, or through a constitutional convention called by two-thirds of state legislatures. Amendments require ratification by three-fourths of states, either through their legislatures or conventions. Constitutional changes can affect the balance of power between the federal government and states, following a process outlined in the Constitution itself. There have been great statesmen who have stood for other views. We will not resurrect the contest. It is now settled by decision. *United States v. Butler, supra.*" (Opinion of the Court on Helvering v. Davis, 1937 by Associate Justice Benjamin Cardozo).

"The conception of the spending power ad-vocated by Hamilton and strongly reinforced by Story has prevailed over that of Madison, which has not been lacking in adherents. Yet difficulties are left when the power is conceded. The line must still be drawn between one welfare and another, between particular and general.

Where this shall be placed cannot be known through a formula in advance of the event. There is a middle ground or certainly a penumbra in which discretion is at large. The discretion, however, is not confided to the courts. The discretion belongs to Congress, unless the choice is clearly wrong, a display of arbitrary power, not an exercise of judgment. This is now familiar law." (Opinion of the Court on Helvering v. Davis, 1937 by Associate Justice Benjamin Cardozo).

Hamilton was no friend to the republic, but a traitor to the republic. The fate of Hamilton served as a reminder to the fate of Caesar. Hamilton, being born outside of the realm of these independent states, never really understood the depth of federalism. Hamilton used the tactic of fear onto the states to strengthen the arrogance of the general government. The court should have listened to the ideas of Madison, the father of the Constitution, not Hamilton, a bureaucrat.

Now the Republic has been presented with an amendment giving that amount of power to the national government and offering an advantage to Mr. Hamilton's writings over Mr. Madison. The matter for now is closed until the national Congress or the sovereign States are presented with an amendment to repeal this unprincipled direct taxation power of the national government.

"Congress did not improvise a judgment when it found that the award of old age benefits would be conducive to the general welfare. The President's Committee on Economic Security made an investigation and report, aided by a research staff of Government officers and employees, and by an advisory Council and seven other advisory groups. Extensive hearings followed before the House Committee on Ways and Means, and the Senate Committee on Finance. A great mass of evidence was brought together supporting the policy which finds expression in the act. Among the relevant facts are these: The number of persons in the United States 65 years of age or over is increasing proportionately as well as absolutely. What is even more important the number of such persons unable to take care of themselves is growing at a threatening pace. More and more our population is becoming urban and industrial instead of rural and agricultural. The evidence is impressive that among industrial workers the younger men and women are preferred over the older." (Opinion of the Court on Helvering v. Davis, 1937 by Associate Justice Benjamin Cardozo).

In the early 20th century and continuing to the present, the national government has increasingly relied on progressive committees and influential progressive groups to shape policies. These policies have had the effect of eroding the principles of federalism that underpin the American Republic, transforming it into a more centralized entity. Justice Cardozo's perspective suggested that the responsibility for addressing these regulatory actions was shifting from the states to the influence of the national

government, potentially impacting the tradition-
al role of individual states.

"The problem is plainly national in area and dimensions. Moreover, laws of the separate states cannot deal with it effectively. Congress, at least, had a basis for that belief. States and local governments are often lacking in the re-sources that are necessary to finance an ade-quate program of security for the aged. This is brought out with a wealth of illustration in recent studies of the problem. Apart from the failure of resources, state and local governments are at times reluctant to increase so heavily the burden of taxation to be borne by their residents for fear of placing themselves in a position of econom-ic disadvantage as compared with neighbors or competitors. We have seen this in our study of the problem of unemployment compensation. A system of old age pensions has special dangers of its own, if put in force in one state and reject-ed in another. The existence of such a system is a bait to the needy and dependent elsewhere, encouraging them to migrate and seek haven of repose. Only a power that is national can serve the interests of all." (Opinion of the Court on Helvering v. Davis, 1937 by Associate Justice Benjamin Cardozo).

Justice Cardozo's stance seemed to align more with the interests of the national government rather than those of the individual states. His perspective appeared to downplay the autonomy and sovereignty of states, which have substantial resources to manage independently. Some argued that it was the federal government's policies that constrained state productivity and autonomy, subjecting them to heavy federal regulations and tax burdens. This, in turn, led to increased dependency on the federal government, ultimately eroding state sovereignty. Justice Cardozo, and most justices of the high court, fail to see the beauty of the states in retaining their sovereignty. They retain their sovereignty to avoid an overwhelming rogue and arrogant national government.

Only an arrogant power that is national can serve the interests of one, not all. It is argued that states might not have faced their current challenges if the national government had allowed them to maintain their sovereignty. The belief is that states would not necessarily have significantly increased their taxation policies, even though they had the authority to do so under the Sixteenth Amendment. Notably, states like Florida, Texas, and Tennessee have managed to keep their tax rates low, including having no state income tax. Many view Justice Cardozo's statement as displaying a degree of arrogance in favor of a planned centralized and autocratic national government. Justice Cardozo and his colleagues may not have fully grasped the essence of the American Republic, characterized by sovereign states. Some argue that there is no system less hazardous than one that allows states to have control. In such a system, if a state does not provide a good quality of life to its citizens, those citizens have the right to move to another state with better conditions, regardless of federal involvement. This principle allows American citizens to seek a better life without becoming dependent on anyone.

Justice Cardozo's perspective, however, contributed to the transformation of the American Republic of sovereign states into a United American Democracy of Dependent States, according to some viewpoints. If only more citizens had been aware of the consequences of the events in 1913 and beyond, they might have fought harder to preserve state sovereignty and independence from federal control. The controversial Sixteenth Amendment might not have been ratified as the supreme law of the land.

"Whether wisdom or unwisdom resides in the scheme of benefits set forth in Title II, it is not for us to say. The answer to such inquiries must come from Congress, not the courts. Our concern here, as often, is with power, not with wisdom. Counsel for respondent has recalled to us the virtues of self-reliance and frugality. There is a possibility, he says, that aid from a paternal government may sap those sturdy virtues and breed a race of weaklings. If Massachusetts so believes and shapes her laws in that conviction, must her breed of sons be changed, he asks, because some other philosophy of government finds favor in the halls of Congress? But the answer is not doubtful. One might ask with equal reason whether the system of protective tariffs is to be set aside at will in one state or another whenever local policy prefers the rule of *laissez faire*. The issue is a closed one. It was fought out long ago. When money is spent to promote the general welfare, the concept of welfare or the opposite is shaped by Congress, not the States. So the concept be not arbitrary, the locality must yield. Constitution, Art VI, Par. 2." (Opinion of the Court on Helvering v. Davis, 1937 by Associate Justice Benjamin Cardozo).

Justice Cardozo's perspective emphasizes the importance of adhering to the proper legislative process. He argues that legislative matters should be handled in the halls of Congress, rather than being subject to judicial writing, amending, or repealing. In the case under discussion, the Court's role is to interpret the law and determine its constitutionality based on the Constitution's provisions. Since the Court applied this law within the framework of the authority granted by the Sixteenth Amendment, it leaves limited room for challenges related to state powers.

Financial Aid from the national government will no doubt in my mind create a nation of weaklings, but dependents first. This truly defeats the purpose of independence and sovereign entities from states to individuals. The national government has no interest in maintaining a prosperous republic in which its common citizenry prospers. The national government's Congress obtained a sanctioned article within the Constitution to be able to place excessive direct taxation directives onto and against the states and then affirmed constitutionally by the court.

States still do have that right to reject a national (direct tax) policy even if it is affirmed by its constitutionality. Justice Cardozo and his fellow progressive-minded thinking individuals do not want to mention the word, "nullification." They want to disavow this word and continue as if Congress passed a supreme law of the land with no sense of checks and balances from the states.

Nobody is talking about *laissez-faire* economics when it comes to the rules of federalism and the Constitution. The protective tariff system was established for the power of the federal government to control but as an indirect tax, never direct. Is it fair to place taxation onto the State of Massachusetts to pay for a bullet train in the States of California or Florida? No. That is the sanctioned robbery amendment at work in creating inequality and chaos. Creating a republic of dependents and not of sovereign citizens. Thus, creating a republic of weaklings, not able to manage their own house. Lincoln was right, a House divided against itself cannot stand. Our American House stands undivided because of its allegiance to the Constitution and sovereign rights among the States.

The concept of the national Congress to provide a general welfare to the states to be relied by the national government is a progressive lie and misinterpretation of this clause. The general government of the United States provides for the general welfare for the protection in international affairs but not in the domestic affairs. The domestic affairs are left unto the states and for the states to work together to form a more perfect union. The ratification of the Sixteenth Amendment in 1913 marked a significant shift in the fiscal powers of the federal government. Prior to this amendment, the federal government primarily relied on indirect taxes, such as tariffs and duties, to generate revenue. The Sixteenth Amendment, however, granted Congress the authority to levy income taxes without the need for apportionment among the states. The progressive movement used the amendment process to establish this vile amendment. Well, we, as constitutionalists, must do the same and propose an amendment to repeal it because it is hurting our republic every day.

The words of Justice Cardozo reflect those of people who share his same progressive ideology. Yes, he stated that Congress has the authority to change the law, but only when a law has attacked the rules of federalism and sovereignty if each State. It then becomes the duty of the court to declare the law unconstitutional.

"*Fifth*. The tax is not invalid as a result of its exemptions. Here again the opinion in *Steward Machine Co. v. Davis, supra*, says all that needs to be said. *Sixth*. The decree of the Court of Appeals should be reversed and that of the District Court affirmed. Reversed." (Opinion of the Court on Helvering v. Davis, 1937 by Associate Justice Benjamin Cardozo).

We should not rely on Court rulings to dictate such tax laws, especially if they are indeed unconstitutional. We rely on the Court itself to properly dictate and interpret the tax law as constitutionally acceptable. I see nothing constitutional on the Social Security Act being labeled as a tax. And for that, I dissent and would have admired the Court, for them to not reverse any action by a lower court and given the power of taxation back to the States.

"Mr. Justice Mc Reynolds and Mr. Justice Butler are of opinion that the provisions of the act here challenged are repugnant to the Tenth

Amendment, and that the decree of the Circuit Court of Appeals should be affirmed." (Dissenting Opinion of the Court on Helvering v. Davis, 1937 by Associate Justices McReynolds and Butler).

Such act in question is not only repugnant, but unprincipled and unconstitutional. It does create a violation to the Tenth Amendment of the Constitution against the sovereignty of the states. It is a sheer violation to establish, not a tax, but let us call it to what it really is, a fee. The federal government has no right to set this tax up and intrude on their sovereignty.

I join with the dissent of this ruling and stand for sovereignty of the states of this American republic.

* * *

Since the creation of the unprincipled Sixteenth Amendment. We have seen the national government create exemptions and tax-loop hole legislation. Prior to 1913, we never saw legislation to better someone or create the illusion of Privilege Under Law.

"Section 310(b)(1) of the Tax Equity and Fiscal Responsibility Act of 1982 removes the federal income tax exemption for interest earned on publicly offered-long-term bonds (hereinafter referred to as bonds) issued by state and local governments (hereinafter referred to collectively as States) unless those bonds are issued in registered (as opposed to bearer) form." (Syllabus of South Carolina v. Baker, Secretary of the Treasury, 1988).

After the national Congress initiated a tax exemption prior to 1982, and now decide to remove it because somebody was not being privileged with loopholes. This is the reason that tax policy, direct tax policy, is best handled at the state level and not the realm of the national government. This constant changing of policy creates mayhem, dismay, and disorder. We cannot have one lenient tax policy and then turn to a more extreme tax one. This – republic was never suited or adopted to have one central tax policy.

Our American republic was not founded to have multiple centralized directive policies under one government. If that were true, we would be continuing to be subjects of the United Kingdom. But let us leave that as it may and discuss the issue at hand – does this law violate the Tenth Amendment to our Constitution and have no issues with the Sixteenth Amendment.

"South Carolina invoked this Court's original jurisdiction, contending that Section 310(b)(1) is constitutionally invalid under the Tenth Amendment and the doctrine of intergovernmental tax immunity." (Syllabus of South Carolina v. Baker, Secretary of the Treasury, 1988).

I think we all can agree that this federal law passed in 1982 and the previous law, are in constant violation to our State Sovereignty doctrine embedded in our Constitution. As it were, our sister states lost a lot of sovereignty in 1913 and sadly, I must rule with the majority opinion of this court's decision. Even though, I am an advocate for state sovereignty first, I am a constitutionalist at heart as it is currently written.

The Tenth Amendment stands higher than some federal tax law but in the eyes of the rogue and arrogant federal government, to them it stands small.

"(a) The Tenth Amendment limits on Congress' authority to regulate state activities are structural, not substantive—that is, the States must find their protection from congressional regulation through the national political process, not through judicially defined spheres of unregulable state activity. In this case, South Carolina has not even alleged that it was deprived of any right to participate in the national political process or that it was singled out in a way that left it politically isolated and powerless. The allegations South Carolina does make—that Congress was uninformed and chose an ineffective remedy—do not amount to an allegation that the political process operated in a defective manner. Pp. 512-513."

(Syllabus of South Carolina v. Baker, Secretary of the Treasury, 1988).

Off-topic, but if the Tenth Amendment places limits on congressional authority based on structural state activities, and not substantive, then one could say that the Interstate Highway Act is an unconstitutional piece of legislation and therefore needs to be recalled, repealed, or nullified by the states.

The infrastructure activities of a state are in no shape or form a part of the national political process. Unless a more than ambitious national senator or national representative wants to apply it to further his own wealth with public taxpayer funds.

The substantive form of state activity that requires congressional authority is what the powers are enumerated for and what the national government strives to dictate.

"Under the intergovernmental tax immunity jurisprudence prevailing at *Pollock's* time, neither the Federal or State Governments could tax income that an individual directly derived from any contract with the other government." (Syllabus of South Carolina v. Baker, Secretary of the Treasury, 1988).

Everything was simpler, prior to 1913, pre-*Pollock*. Everything went downhill when congressional authority started to meddle in state activities and affairs.

But the court is correct in saying that before these times, neither government had any right to pass direct tax directives among each other. All that changed, with the unprincipled and unscrupulous Sixteenth Amendment.

"Because. By hypothesis, Section 310 effectively prohibits issuing unregistered bonds, it presents the very situation FERC distinguished from commandeering of state regulatory machinery: the extent to which the Tenth Amendment "shields the States from generally applicable federal regulations." 456 U.S., at 759. Section 310 regulates state activities; it does not, as did the statute in FERC, seek to control or influence the manner in which States regulate private parties. The NGA nonetheless contends that Section 310 has commandeered the state legislative and administrative process because many state legislatures had to amend a substantial manner of statute in order to issue bonds in registered form and because state officials had to devote substantial effort to determine how best to implement a registered bond system. Such "commandeering" is, however an inevitable consequence of regulating state activity. Any federal regulation demands compliance." (Opinion of the Court of South Carolina v. Baker, Secretary of the Treasury by Associate Justice William J. Brennan, 1988).

The national government has "commandeered" every action against the states, post-1913. Every action commandeered by the general government is an action of unconstitutional proportions. They have shown contempt for our rules of federalism and individual state sovereignty that builds this American republic.

"Any federal regulation demands compliance." This is how the federal government has made its compliance. They forget their enumerated powers, with increasing power they add themselves, believe that they control everything. Not all federal regulation demands compliance, but all sovereign States demand to be non-compliant. This is just another example of how rogue and arrogant the federal government has become toward federalism and its States.

"That a State wishing to engage in certain activity must take administrative and sometimes legislative action to commonplace that presents no constitutional defect. After *Garcia*, for example, several States and municipalities had to take administrative and legislative action to comply with the wage and overtime provisions of the Federal Labor Standards Act." (Opinion of the Court of South Carolina v. Baker, Secretary of the Treasury by Associate Justice William J. Brennan, 1988).

The Supreme Court's ruling in the Garcia v. San Antonio Metropolitan Transit Authority (1985) case addressed the application of federal labor laws to state and local government employees. In that decision, the Court determined that federal labor laws, such as the Fair Labor Standards Act (FLSA), are applicable to state and local governments as employers. This ruling was an expansion of federal authority over state and local governments in the realm of labor regulation, citing the Supremacy Clause of the Constitution. As the federal government forces the sovereign States to comply for an unconstitutional national law standard, you are forcing them into tyranny. National Labor law standards are just as unconstitutional as a national immigration law standard. States are bound to refuse to cooperate, and the high court should know this regardless of what Chief Justice Taney inscribed in his racist and arrogant opinions.

"Indeed, even the pre-*Garcia* line of the Tenth Amendment cases recognized that Congress could constitutionally impose federal requirements on States that States could meet only by amending their statutes. See *EEOC v. Wyoming*, 460 U.S. 226, 253-254, and n. 2 (1983) (Burger, C. J., dissenting) (citing state statutes from over half the States that did not comply with the federal statute upheld by the Court). Under NGA's theory, moreover, any State could immunize its activities from federal regulation by simply codifying the manner in which it engages in those activities. In short, the NGA's theory of "commandeering" would not only render *Garcia* a nullity, but would also restrict congressional regulation of state activities even more tightly that it was restricted under the now overruled *National League of Cities* line of cases. We find the theory foreclosed by precedent, and uphold the constitutionality of Section 310 under the Tenth Amendment." (Opinion of the Court of South Carolina v. Baker, Secretary of the Treasury by Associate Justice William J. Brennan, 1988).

That is not how this republic was established to have been formed. The federal government is no position to place requirements onto the states especially if they are unconstitutional and unprincipled. Furthermore, for a state to be forced into compliance to fit into the requirements of the national standard is beyond tyrannical.

But as this ruling is applied to federal tax policies, then yes, unfortunately, states must comply. But the high court needs to be specific in its language. Because of that, it is open to misinterpretation and with misinterpretation comes more of a legal mess than a civics mess.

"South Carolina contends that even if a statute banning state bearer bonds entirely would be constitutional, Section 310 unconstitutionally violates the doctrine of intergovernmental tax immunity because it imposes a tax on the interest earned on a state bond. We agree with South Carolina that Section 310 is inconsistent with *Pollock v. Farmers' Loan & Trust Co.*, 157 U.S. 429 (1895), which held that any interest earned on a state bond was immune from federal taxation." (Opinion of the Court of South Carolina v. Baker, Secretary of the Treasury by Associate Justice William J. Brennan, 1988).

I do not believe that any sovereign State, would be contended in having a ban on state barrier bonds. What a small majority of sovereign States would be contended as to see bring an end to the Sixteenth Amendment. If individuals living in states where the tax structure is at its highest, they would understand that the direct tax policies are a state enumerated power. Therefore, they would be inclined to support a repeal of this vile amendment. I am speaking to you, California, New York, New Jersey, Colorado, Illinois.

Of course, Section 310 is inconsistent with the 1895 *Pollock* ruling. Back then, there was constitutional restraint for the general government in imposing a direct tax or any tax policy onto the States. *Pollock* cannot longer be applied because of the sanctioned robbery amendment.

What is wrong with the sovereign states of today? Have they failed to read the Constitution and past rulings? This is part of the major problem that is happening to our republic. When there is a threat to our federalism republic, there is little action to be done by the states, and when it becomes too late. It is too late to cry over spilled milk. But the solution is not to sweep the milk away, but to clean it right up. Repeal is the cleaning solution. Laziness becomes ignorance and ignorance becomes filled with unconstitutional despair. This happened in 2016, in where individuals and states found unconstitutional despair under President Trump, and it got nothing but more of a rogue and arrogant federal government.

"The Secretary and the Master, however, suggest that we should uphold the constitutionality of Section 310 does not abolish the tax exemption for state bond interest entirely but rather taxes the interest on state bonds only if the bonds are not issued in the form that Congress requires. In our view, however, this suggestion implicitly rests on a rather mischievous proposition of law. If, for example, Congress imposed a tax that applied exclusively on South Carolina and levied the tax directly on the South Carolina treasury, we would be obligated to adjudicate the constitutionality of that tax even if Congress allowed South Carolina to escape the tax by restructuring its state government in a way Congress found more to its liking. The United States cannot convert an unconstitutional tax into a constitutional one simply by making the tax conditional. Whether Congress could have imposed the condition by direct regulation is irrelevant; Congress cannot employ unconstitutional means to reach a constitutional end. Under Pollock, a tax on the interest income derived from any state bond was considered a direct tax on the State and thus unconstitutional. 157 U.S., at 585-586. If this constitutional rule still applies, Congress cannot threaten to tax the interest on state bonds that do not conform to congressional dictates. We thus decline to follow a suggestion that would force us to embrace implicitly a proposition of law far more controversial than the current validity of Pollock's ban on taxing state bond interest, and proceed to address whether Pollock should be explicitly overruled." (Opinion of the Court of South Carolina v. Baker, Secretary of the Treasury by Associate Justice William J. Brennan, 1988).

The federal government's executive branch suggests that the Court upholds the constitutionality of Section 310. I quite frankly agree with them, only because the executive branch has received authorization from Congress that they have that right under the amendment. Post-1913, Congress has the power to impose any direct tax onto any sovereign State, without being apportioned. So, let's spare this charade of a statement from Justice Brennan.

It is quite relevant to Congress' means of imposing a tax. In this case, Congress does have a means to reach a constitutional end due because of the Sixteenth Amendment. Anything else not enumerated in the Constitution, Congress has no right to impose or force compliance to obtain a constitutional end onto the sovereign states.

To lay to rest this question regarding the *Pollock* decision. *Pollock* was superseded by the Sixteenth, and yet remains inconsistent. As *Pollock* remains the opinion of the land, and ruling precedent that restrained the federal government on a sanctioned robbery scheme. A court ruling is simply the rule of the land, not the law of the land. The rule of the land can be changed, especially when there is nothing constitutional about it.

Then came the initiation of the Sixteenth Amendment legislation, and as it passed the ratification process by Republican progressive corrupt bargains. The newly added amendment sealed the fate of the 1895 ruling and overruled it. There is no need to address the ruling, it has been overruled since 1913. The only way this ruling comes back to life is if we repeal this dreadful amendment and re-apply it to our

American Republic of sovereign states. Until then, the Sixteenth remains the law of the land.

We need to bring awareness to the American people of this travesty imposed by then Republican Progressives of the early Twentieth century. Now being continually supportive by the Democrat progressives of the Twenty-first century.

This has created a gateway of hellish fire with unapportion, unrestrained and unregulated tax and spending legislation. Legislation to appease the populist crowd during an election cycle and in the first 100 days of a president's first four- year term in office.

I will continue to oppose any fiscal and tax legislation being presented to the national Congress that is set forth to be unapportion across these states. I know we believe that all these legislative actions are bounded by the Constitution, but in theory and practice remain unprincipled and not set in the ways of federalism.

This 1982 fiscal tax that Congress imposed onto the states just creates mayhem because of the unbelievable amendment in question.

"We then stated: "Where, as here, the economic but not the legal incidence of the tax falls upon the Federal Government, such a tax generally does not violate the constitutional immunity if it does not discriminate against holders of federal property or those with whom the Federal Government deals." Ibid. (emphasis added)."

(Opinion of the Court of South Carolina v. Baker, Secretary of the Treasury by Associate Justice William J. Brennan, 1988).

"TEFRA Section 310 thus clearly imposes no direct tax on the States. The tax is imposed on and collected from the bondholders, not States in implementing the registration system are not "taxes" within the meaning of the tax immunity doctrine. Nor does Section 310 discriminate against the States. The provisions of Section 310 seek to assure that all publicly offered long-term bonds are issued in registered form, whether issued by state or local governments, the Federal Government, or private corporations. See supra, at 510." (Opinion of the Court of South Carolina v. Baker, Secretary of the Treasury by Associate Justice William J. Brennan, 1988).

"Removing the tax exemption for interest earned on state bonds would not, moreover, create a discrimination between state and corporate bond interest is already subject to federal tax." (Opinion of the Court of South Carolina v. Baker, Secretary of the Treasury by Associate Justice William J. Brennan, 1988).

"Because the federal imposition of a bond registration requirement on States does not violate the Tenth Amendment and because a nondiscriminatory federal tax on the interest earned on state bonds does not violate the intergovernmental tax immunity doctrine, we uphold the constitutionality of Section 310(b)(1), overrule the exceptions to the Special Master's Report, and approve his recommendation to enter judgment for the defendant. It is so ordered." (Opinion of the Court of South Carolina v. Baker, Secretary of the Treasury by Associate Justice William J. Brennan, 1988).

Any federal tax policy, whether direct or indirect and of course unapportion, is a direct tax upon its sovereign states and its citizens. I am not defining the word "discrimination" in the sense of racial or sexist discrimination in how the high court is trying to define this word in this paragraph statement.

It is showing discrimination between the sovereign states in population and census apportionment. That was the entire point in stating that the central government was not cut out to be apportioning direct tax laws across the several States. In theory and in practice, it is impossible.

In the American Republic colonial days, you could not compare the size of the cities of Philadelphia, Pennsylvania, New York City, New York to cities like Charleston, South Carolina or Alexandria, Virginia. The differences in census were quite different and it is just the same as the cities of New York City, New York to Denver, Colorado.

So, I believe in this aspect Section 310 does show a distinct hint of discrimination. But the national government has been dictating discriminatory policies across our several states. Whether it was racial discrimination, sexist discrimination. And now they have shown their true colors of federalism discrimination.

The opinion of the court ruling does sound quite fitting to the Constitution. But it is not quite up to the standards of the Constitutional Framers' words in how they crafted this principled document.

The only person that I feel comfortable in relying on to draw a credible and true constitutional concluding concurring decision on the *SC v. Baker* ruling, is the man who served this high court with distinguished honors from 1986 to his untimely death in 2016. This man truly knew the rules of federalism that rightly defined our republic between the national government and its sovereign states.

"I join in the Court's judgment, and in its opinion except for Part II. I do not join the latter because, as observed by THE CHIEF JUSTICE, post at 529-530, it unnecessarily casts doubt upon FERC v. Mississippi, 456 U.S. 742 (1982), and because it misdescribes the holding of Garcia v. San Antonio Metropolitan Transit

Authority, 469 U.S. 528 (1985). I do not read Garcia as adopting—in fact I read it as explicitly disclaiming—the proposition attributed to it in today's opinion, ante, at 512-513, that the "national political process" is the States' only constitutional protection, and that nothing except the demonstration of "some extraordinary defects" in the operation of that process can justify judicial relief. We said in Garcia: "These cases do not require us to identify or define what affirmative limits the constitutional structure might impose on federal action affecting the States under the Commerce Clause. I agree only that that structure does not prohibit what the Federal Government has done here."
(Concurring Opinion of the Court of South Carolina v. Baker, Secretary of the Treasury, Associate Justice Antonin Scalia, 1988).

The late Justice Scalia was indeed in a class of his own of judicial constitutionalism. When the opinion of the court made so-called relevant references to the case in discussion, Scalia always found federalism in his opinions to make his point clear. He always minimized the role of the federal government where it was spreading its unconstitutionality across the sovereign states, while still recognizing its proper enumerated powers.

A federal public utilities act of Congress is not the same as what this case entailed. The case of *FERC v. Mississippi*, 1982, was a suit brought by a state utilities company that the federal government was encroaching onto a sovereign state's powers. Sadly, the progressives in the court at that time, decided to adapt a public utility into the Commerce Clause. As we all know, the Mississippi owned public utilities was not crossing into another state for commerce, and if it were, the national government has no right to regulate it. The same goes for *Garcia v. Metropolitan Transit Authority*, 1985, in where these cases unjustly and unconstitutionally justified under the Constitution's Commerce Clause. Scalia saw no good in comparison to *SC v. Baker* and I quite agree with him.

"I agree only that that structure does not prohibit what the Federal Government has done here, former Associate Justice Antonin Scalia. In that sense, Scalia was always a literal constitutionalist at heart.

I also quite agree that the newly added enumerated powers dictated in the Sixteenth Amendment and with the current legal case and affirmed in the ruling are quite constitutional. The 1982 act that led to this case, is justified by the Sixteenth Amendment for Congress to pass un-apportion, unregulated and unrestrained taxation policies onto the States. To show the regulation enforcement against the States is unconstitutional. A State can refuse to cooperate with union officials and still retain their sovereignty and allegiance to the Constitution. Regardless to what nine unelected federal government bureaucrats state. I only side with SC v. Baker and with Justice Scalia because they showed true federalism in his words to express what is constitutional and what is not in today's ruling.

I see a major issue in Justice Sandra Day O'Connor's dissenting opinion in this ruling, and that is that it is contradicting the Constitution. As much as I would like to see the court contradict and overrule an unprincipled amendment, I must stand by the Constitution. It is Congress that proposes to repeal amendments, not the court.

"I believe that state autonomy is an important factor to be considered in reviewing the National Government's exercise of its enumerated powers." (Dissenting Opinion of the Court of South Carolina v. Baker, Secretary of the Treasury by Associate Justice Sandra Day O'Connor, 1988).

I always consider the constitutional role of state autonomy over the defined powers of the federal government. But when the Constitution has defined the role of the national government regarding the role of taxation and fiscal policies, then the role of state autonomy becomes diminished. It is a shame that the progressives of that time, and progressives of today fails to recognize the rules of federalism and way this republic has been established to be governed.

"I dissent from the decision to overrule Pollock v. Farmers' Loan & Trust Co., 157 U.S. 429 (1895), and I would invalidate Congress' attempt to regulate the sovereign States by threatening to deprive them of this tax immunity, which would increase their dependence on the National Government." (Dissenting Opinion of the Court of South Carolina v. Baker, Secretary of the Treasury by Associate Justice Sandra Day O'Connor, 1988).

> "I agree only that that structure does not prohibit what the Federal Government has done here." – Associate Justice Antonin Scalia

This case did not overrule *Pollock*. The Sixteenth Amendment overruled *Pollock* and gave precedent to the federal government. This case just stated the fact that Congress has the authority to overrule or codify rulings by way of congressional acts or amendments.

"I agree only that that structure does not prohibit what the Federal Government has done here." – Associate Justice Antonin Scalia.

Scalia's words of federalism wisdom and advice speak stronger than O'Connor's dissent. You can still believe in state sovereignty when you also recognize the powers of each governmental entity.

The sad thing is that this republic has changed from an American republic of sovereign states to a United American democratic of dependent States. We have lost our state sovereignty to be state dependency. We strove to become a new nation away from centralized autocracy, to become the very thing we were supposed to gain independence in 1776.

The establishment of the Sixteenth Amendment along with the creation of the Federal Reserve, a.k.a., Central Bank, made America into a dependent nation. The increase of dependency keeps on growing at every minute of our lives and it is not going to stop until the state say enough and refuse to cooperate and end this dependency.

The overwhelming dependency will not end, as we just saw recently with President Biden giving federal funds to dependents on their education loans. But the sheer dependency shown by President Biden did not start there and will not end there. The Trump presidency showed nothing but bringing dependency onto the States. From federal border-wall building to extending the federal stimulus.

The increase sentiment of dependency has ever increased since before since its inception of 1929. Before the stock market felt the crash, it was feeling the rogue and arrogance from the national government. It was the dependency of the federal government that lead to the crash inflicting dismay upon the sovereign States and their citizens. After the crash, and the election of Franklin D. Roosevelt is where we saw an increase in the dependency sentiment and we have not been able to retreat from it or nullify it.

Then came the age of Eisenhower in where we saw a massive increased dependency from the federal government. And that gave the New Frontier of John F. Kennedy an excuse to continue it and expand it more under the Great Society of Lyndon B. Johnson. From a beginning of social programs under the realm of the national government that started to increase the federal debt.

The era of Richard M. Nixon continued with those social programs, but also extended the housing situation and expanded its dependent role into ours States' environmental issues. Then came the era of Ronald Reagan, where he cut those federal pesky social programs and placed those federal funds into Wall Street.

Placing those federal funds in useless social programs into a batch of privateers is just more of the same arrogance of the rogue federal government.

During the southern charm era of William J. Clinton, we did see a slight increase of social dependency but that ended in 1995. For the first time since the New Deal programs, the federal government saw a cut in spending and a giant surplus in the national treasury. But that surplus came to an end once again with the era of George W. Bush, who oversawan increas in spending – from elusive national protective custody of The Patriot Act to yet again more social spending, in particularly education spending. In the eight years of the second Bush dynasty presidency, it appears he was guided more by LBJ and by FDR, rather than Madison or Jefferson.

The era of Barack Obama became extremely rogue and arrogant with no hint of protecting federalism. We entered a new age of dependency with national government's health protective custody.

Neither the Trump presidency, nor the Biden presidency, have done anything differently. They continued the same rogue and arrogant attitude of dependency policy onto the states.

To disavow the paragraph statement of former Justice O'Connor, the States have now become dependent of the federal government. Overruling of *Pollock* is just the continuing game of this era of dependency. The solution in stopping this game is to yet again find a way to repeal the amendment in question, and that will finally bring an end to state dependency.

"In my view, the Tenth Amendment and principles of federalism inherent in the Constitution prohibit Congress from taxing or threatening to tax the interest paid on state and

municipal bonds. It is also arguable that the States' autonomy is protected from substantial federal incursions by virtue of the Guarantee Clause of the Constitution, Art. IV, Section 4."
(Dissenting Opinion of the Court of South Carolina v. Baker, Secretary of the Treasury by Associate Justice Sandra Day O'Connor, 1988).

In my humble, constitutional scholar mind, the Tenth Amendment should stomp over the Sixteenth Amendment but that is not how the Constitution functions in what remain of our American republic. The way this republic was established, we are a union of federal states, as Calhoun stated it. The Guarantee Clause is just another right left up to the states to enforce, while the national government remains an arbitrator.

But the progressives that obtained national power and populist attention disavowed certain sovereign guaranteed rights and got power into their hands and away from the states. But states lost partial, if not all their sovereignty, with the passage and ratification of the Sixteenth and Seventeenth Amendments. Regarding the

Sixteenth Amendment, it allows the national Congress to pass unapportion taxation policy on to the sovereign states at their own lawful indiscretion. It is an unfortunate legitimate price the States had to pay to obtain this amendment into our Constitution.

"State and local governments rely heavily on borrowed funds to finance education, road construction, and utilities, among other purposes. As the Court recognizes, States will have to increase the interest rates they pay on bonds by 28-35% if the interest is subject to the federal income tax." (Dissenting Opinion of the Court of South Carolina v. Baker, Secretary of the Treasury by Associate Justice Sandra Day O'Connor, 1988).

There is nothing new with this statement from Justice O'Connor. As Justice O'Connor stated before, we recognize that we have become a dependent of the federal government. With that dependency comes unapportion direct taxation, spending, and unprincipled mayhem.

When a state becomes beholden to the federal government and accepts aid, it becomes beholden to unconstitutional demands, not requests.

"In upholding the application of the federal income tax to income derived from a state lease, this court decided that mere theoretical concerns about interference with the functions of government did not justify immunity, but the "[r]egard must be had to substance and direct effects." *Helvering v. Mountain Producers Corp.*, 303 U.S. 376, 386 (1938). In *Helvering v. Gerhardt*, 304 U.S. 405 (1938), this Court upheld the application of the federal income tax to income earned by a state employee, because there is "[no] immunity when the burden on the state is so speculative and uncertain that if allowed it would restrict the federal taxing power without affording any corresponding tangible protection to the state government. *Id.*, at 419-420."
(Dissenting Opinion of the Court of South Carolina v. Baker, Secretary of the Treasury by Associate Justice Sandra Day O'Connor, 1988).

The courts in modern times have done as always, usurping their powers. Granting immunity or not granting immunity is only the concern of the actions of Congress, not the Court.

"The instant case differs critically from the cases quoted above because the Special Master found that, if the interest on state and local bonds is taxed, the cost of borrowing by state and local governments would rise substantially. This certainly would affect seriously state and local government operations. The majority is unconcerned with this difference because it is satisfied with the formal test of intergovernmental tax immunity that can be distilled from later cases. Under this test, if a tax is not imposed directly on the government, and does not discriminate against the government, then it does not violate intergovernmental tax immunity." See *ante*, at 523." (Dissenting Opinion of the Court of South Carolina v. Baker, Secretary of the Treasury by Associate Justice Sandra Day O'Connor, 1988).

The whole point of the Republican progressive movement's push for direct taxation was to make it into an amendment. With that amendment comes unrestrained fiscal policy onto and against the sovereign states.

Injustice to any state's sovereignty is a threat to state sovereignty everywhere. Justice O'Connor's statement regarding that federal taxation imposing onto state activities would be indeed a threat to state sovereignty. That would not even come to play if to play if we did not have a Sixteenth Amendment. The sad fact is that there is a despicable authority clause in the Constitution to impose financial tyranny and burden onto the states. And the Framers had no intention of placing that burden.

I do believe that Justice O'Connor is misquoting and misinterpreting the words of Chief Justice Marshall – no friend of federalism, but a friend of autocracy. The court opinion of *McCullough* was a decision to increase the size of the national government. Even though, this opinion did not give authorization for the creation of a central bank, it still showed restraint toward the sovereign states to further allow their own financial choices of own legislation.

I do not see a defense of state sovereignty from Justice O'Connor when quoting the first Chief Justice of the high court. He did not hold back in expanding the role of the federal government with more unprecedented and unconstitutional power. May I remind my fellow readers and followers that this was the Chief Justice that expanded the role of the court in judicial review to every single aspect of legislation in its infamous and unprincipled decisions known as *Marbury v. Madison*, 1803. This is where I distrust Marshall. I should never quote him in anything for support of federalism or individual state sovereignty.

Justice Holmes in paraphrasing this quote from Marshall, I find to be less egregious and arrogant only because the Court must abide by its Sixteenth Amendment to the Constitution. I would find it more rogue and arrogant if the Court would disavow the Sixteenth and find ways to diminish or repeal it. It is not their duty to sort out these actions. Their powers are not to create or establish tax policy but interpret them as just, as they did with the Revenue Act of 1913.

I find the Holmes quote a little bit more constitutional than the Marshall quote. Marshall had no constitutional backing to advise the federal government on a power of direct taxation, which was non-existent. While with the Holmes quote, it is more constitutional. I'd say more constitutional than principled because I truly still believe the power of direct taxation lies only with the states.

I also believe the Tenth Amendment also means something to a strong constitutionalist scholar like myself and my fellow readers. There are certain rights of the Tenth that have been relinquished to the powers of taxation by the general government, unfortunately.

I would want one day for some ambitious, courageous and constitutionalist State Legislator from a strong admiring sovereign state to initiate a resolution amendment to finally be rid of the stranglehold of the Sixteenth Amendment. We cannot rely on the court to declare a national constitutional amendment unholy and unconstitutional. It must be done by the action of the sovereign states, respectively the people.

I truly find no support in Justice O'Connor's dissent only because she is fighting a losing battle in the Court. This battle is fought in the legislative fields of our beloved American republic of sovereign states.

"Federal taxation of state activities is inherently a threat to state sovereignty. As Chief Justice Marshall observed long ago, "the power to tax involves the power to destroy." *McCullough v. Maryland*, 4 Wheat. 316, 431 (1819). Justice Holmes later qualified this principle, observing that "[t]he power to tax is not the power to destroy while this Court sits." *Panhandle Oil Co., v. Mississippi ex rel. Knox*, 277 U.S. 218, 223 (1928) (Holmes J., joined by Brandeis and Stone, JJ., dissenting). If this Court is the States' sole protector against the threat of crushing taxation, it must take seriously its responsibility to sit in judgement of federal tax initiatives. I do not think that the Court has lived up to its constitutional role in this case. The Court has failed to enforce the constitutional safeguards of state autonomy and self-sufficiency that may be found in the Tenth Amendment and the Guarantee Clause, as well as in the principles of federalism implicit in the Constitution. I respectfully dissent." (Dissenting Opinion of the Court of South Carolina v. Baker, Secretary of the Treasury by Associate Justice Sandra Day O'Connor, 1988).

I dissent to her dissent, only because it shares no true voice for federalism. But I share no victorious glory in supporting this court's opinion. It is a constitutional opinion, but not a principled one.

The only opinion I share with enthusiasm was the concurring opinion of Justice Scalia. At least this opinion showed constitutional and principled wisdom towards the taxation structure of our republic. He was critical of the following judgment comparisons that the opinion of the court made while stating the fact. The fact was that this type of ruling showed federal government precedent within its law in question.

The precedent is the Sixteenth Amendment and that is the authority granted to the federal government. If this law would have been adopted prior to 1895, then the Constitution stands for state sovereignty. But alas, post-1895 to 1913, the Constitution stands with autocracy. Scalia stated a clear judgment of true constitutional judicial activism and always abided by the rules of federalism. We all must abide and apply federalism across our American republic because that is the last thing it binds us together as a more perfect union of sovereign states. Even when the Constitution contradicts the federalism ideals of our republic, we must always stand true to our Constitution and its meaning of federalism and state sovereignty.

As I have read the court cases and laws passed after the adoption of the Sixteenth Amendment, I have concluded that this Amendment shall be aptly named, The Sanctioned Robbery Amendment.

It is an Amendment that has granted extreme unconstitutional powers to the Congress and validated unprincipledly by the Court to pass and not pass any sources of income to be taxed. The Congress, in its present form, has been very adapted to the adoption of the Sixteenth Amendment and have done nothing to alleviate the situation for the several states and its people.

Hence, why my first two chapters are discussions of the other unprincipled Amendment that has taken away the independence and sovereignty of the several states, while also increasing the power of the federal government through this unprincipled Amendment.

But I feel the fight is far from over for the American people. I believe that we can regain our state powers if we put our faith, money, and influence in repealing these mess of unprincipled Amendments that is dismantling our American republic of sovereign States.

BIBLIOGRAPHY

CHAPTER I

The Election of Senators, Haynes, George H., Ph. D., Henry Holt and Company, 1906.

CHAPTER II

The Election of Senators, Haynes, George H., Ph. D., Henry Holt and Company, 1906.

Calvin Coolidge and the Moral Case for Economy, Amity Shlaes, author of Coolidge, Imprimis, a publication of Hillsdale College, February 2013, Vol., 42, Number 2.

The Contested Senate Election of William Scott Vare, Samuel J. Astorino, 1961

The Vanishing Rights of the States: A Discussion of the Right of the Senate to Nullify the Action of a Sovereign State in the Selection of its Representatives in the Senate, James M. Beck, L.L.D; New York George H. Doran Company, 1926.

There have been 12 U.S. senators indicted while in office. Here's a list; Terence Samuel, The Washington Post, April 2, 2015

Opinion of the Court of Trinsey v. Pennsylvania; United States Court of Appeals. Third District, by Chief Judge Sloviter, 1991

Illinois governor charged with taking bribes for Obama's Senate seat, Elana Schor in Washington, The Guardian, December 9, 2008.

Ben Sasse Calls for Repealing the 17th Amendment, Eliminating Popular-Vote Senate Elections; Brittany Bernstein, September 9, 2020

CHAPTER III

Syllabus of Pollock v. Farmers' Loan and Trust Company, 1895.

Rehearing of Pollock v. Farmers' Loan and Trust Company, 1895.

Dissenting Opinion of Pollock v. Farmers' Loan and Trust Company by Associate Justice John Marshall Harlan, 1895.

Opinion of the Court of Pollock v. Farmers' Loan and Trust Company by Associate Justice Chief Justice Melville Fuller, 1895

CHAPTER IV

Syllabus of South Carolina v. Baker, Secretary of the Treasury, 1988

Appellant Argument of Stanton v. Baltic Mining Company by Mr. Charles A. Snow, 1916)

Opinion of the Court on Helvering v. Davis, 1937 by Associate Justice Benjamin Cardozo

Dissenting Opinion of the Court on Helvering v. Davis, 1937 by Associate Justices McReynolds and Butler

Opinion of the Court of South Carolina v. Baker, Secretary of the Treasury by Associate Justice William J. Brennan, 1988

Concurring Opinion of the Court of South Carolina v. Baker, Secretary of the Treasury, Associate Justice Antonin Scalia, 1988

Dissenting Opinion of the Court of South Carolina v. Baker, Secretary of the Treasury by Associate Justice Sandra

LISTEN ON SPREAKER, SPOTIFY,
I HEART RADIO, GOOGLE PODCASTS
STATES RIGHTS RADIO
E-Mail: statesrightsradio@mail.com
Website: *www.statessovereignty.org*
Instagram: states.rights.radio